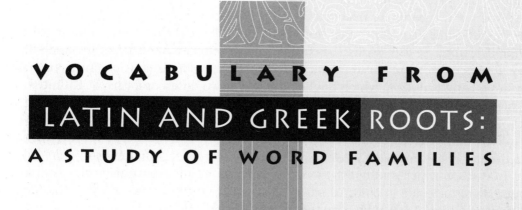

VOCABULARY FROM
LATIN AND GREEK ROOTS:
A STUDY OF WORD FAMILIES

By: Elizabeth Osborne

Edited by Paul Moliken
Illustrated by Larry Knox

Prestwick House wishes to extend its gratitude to the many contributors whose assistance, comments, and expertise were essential in completing this book.

PRESTWICK HOUSE, INC.
"Everything for the English Classroom!"

P.O. Box 658 • Clayton, DE 19938
Tel: 1.800.932.4593 • Web site: www.prestwickhouse.com

ISBN 978-1-58049-200-3

INTRODUCTION

Prestwick House developed *Vocabulary from Latin and Greek Roots* in response to numerous requests for a solid etymology-based vocabulary program. Because the aim of the program is to increase retention of new words as well as to expand students' vocabulary, we chose to organize the units by meaning rather than alphabetically. A student who associates a root with an idea will be more likely to correctly assess the definition of that root's English derivative.

Each unit contains four Latin and/or Greek roots; two to four English vocabulary words are provided for each root. Unit 7 (PAGE) of this book, for instance, contains four roots have to do with writing, words and letters. When a student reaches the first root in this Unit. he or she will see the key letters that signal the presence of the root in an English word: SCRIB, SCRIPT. Beneath the key letters is the root from which the English is derived. Students will notice that there are sometimes two forms of the root, and sometimes one. The inclusion of two forms indicates a Latin verb from which English has taken two different forms. SCRIBERE, for instance, gives us scribble, meaning "to write sloppily," while SCRIPTUS gives us script, meaning "writing, something written." When a root comes from a Latin adjective or noun, only one form will generally be included. Greek roots also appear in only one form.

Beneath the definition of the root, the student will find the word, its pronunciation, part of speech, and English definition. In cases in which an English word has multiple meanings, we have chosen to include only the meaning appropriate to the grade level for which the book is intended. The word course in this book, then, is a verb meaning "to flow, to rush" rather than a noun meaning "class;" in Book III, *pedestrian* means "ordinary" rather than "a traveler on foot." In some instances, students may find it useful to review meanings that do not appear and discuss how they are related to the meaning presented.

If the word has a prefix, or if it is especially difficult to reconcile with its root, the entry will contain an analysis of the parts of the word, followed by a literal definition. *Repulsion* in Book III, Unit Five, is explained as *re*, meaning "back," + *pulsum*; the literal meaning is "a pushing back."

Finally, each entry provides a sentence using the word and introduces pertinent synonyms and/or antonyms. For added visual reinforcement of this understanding, mnemonic cartoons appear in each Unit.

Six different kinds of exercise follow the Unit entries. They include three kinds of practice using words in context, one test of a student's ability to infer information based on a word's meaning, one reading comprehension exercise, and one activity in which a student must deduce the meaning of an unfamiliar word based on knowledge of the word's root. By the end of the exercises in each Unit, students will have had thorough practice using the word in context and will be prepared to make the word part of their working vocabulary.

We hope that you find the *Vocabulary from Latin and Greek Roots* series effective in teaching new words and in fostering student interest in the history of our fascinating language.

Note: A guide to the pronunciation symbols and a list of Latin and Greek prefixes can be found at the beginning of this book.

PREFIXES

A (L.) away from

A (G.) not, no

AB (L.) away from

AD (L.) toward

ALTER (L.) another

AMPHI (G.) around, both

ANA (G.) up

ANTE (L.) before

ANTI (G.) against

CIRCUM (L.) around

CO (L.) with, together

CON (L.) with, together

CONTRA (L.) against

DE (L.) down, down from

DIA (G.) through

DIS (L.) apart, away from

DYS (G.) bad

E (L.) out of

EC (G.) outside

EM (G.) in, within

EN (G.) in, within

EPI (G.) upon

EX (L.) out of, away from *

HYPER (G.) over

IN (L.) in, into, on, against, not

INTRO (L.) inside

OB (L.) against

OMNI (L.) every, all

PER (L.) through

PERI (G.) around

POST (L.) after

PRE (L.) before

RE (L.) back, again *

RETRO (L.) backwards

SUB (L.) beneath

SUPER, SUR (L.) above

SYM (G.) with, together

SYN (G.) with, together

TRANS (L.) across

TELE (G.) distant

* Note: *re, ex, con* and *in* sometimes serve as *intensifiers*. In such cases, these prefixes simply mean *very*.

PRONUNCIATION GUIDE

a = tr**a**ck

ā = m**a**te

ä = f**a**ther

â = c**a**re

e = p**e**t

ē = b**e**

i = b**i**t

ī = b**i**te

o = j**o**b

ō = wr**o**te

ô = p**o**rt

ōō = pr**oo**f

u = p**u**n

ū = **you**

û = p**u**rr

ə = **a**bout, syst**e**m, s**u**pper, circ**u**s

WORD LIST FOR BOOK I

UNIT 1
affection
agenda
coagulate
cooperate
deficient
defunct
facsimile
inoperable
malfunction
operational
petrify
suffice
transact

UNIT 2
circumstance
composition
constant
deposit
impermanent
opponent
proposition
remnant
stationary
status

UNIT 3
apprehend
assumption
capacity
captivate
comprehend
consume
presumptuous
rapidity
rapture
recipient
sumptuous

UNIT 4
convict
domestic
domicile
dominate
dominion
evict
omnipotent
possessive
potent
regal
regicide
reign
victorious

UNIT 5
adjacent
appendix
ballistic
dispense
encompass
parable
passable
projectile
subject
suspend
symbolize

UNIT 6
absolute
conservative
constrict
deliverance
liberal
liberate
observant
preservation
restriction
solution

UNIT 7
analogy
apologetic
biographical
descriptive
diagram
illogical
literal
literate
manuscript
obliterate
program
subscribe

UNIT 8
accessible
ambition
course
currency
gradual
occurrence
procession
progression
recurrent
succession
transgress
transit

UNIT 9
affirmative
confirm
disintegrate
effortless
evaluate
fortify
fortitude
infirm
integrate
integrity
invalid
invaluable
validate

UNIT 10
compute
confidante
confident
creed
discredit
incredible
reputation
sensation
sensible
sentimental

UNIT 11
accompaniment
asocial
associate
companionship
host
hostile
militant
militarize
sociable
socialize

UNIT 12
capitalize
decapitate
emancipate
linguistic
manual
manufacture
multilingual
oral
oration
oratory

UNIT 13
celebrant
celebratory
celebrity
delude
exhilarating
frugal
fruitful
hilarity
illusion
jubilant
jubilee

UNIT 14
application
complex
dismantle
duplicate
mantle
reveal
textile
texture
unveil

UNIT 15
abduct
attractive
conduct
contract
convection
distract
produce
prosecute
sequel
sequence
vehicle

UNIT 16
alleviate
brutality
brute
elevate
grave
gravity
impress
leverage
levitate
oppress

UNIT 17
abbreviate
attentive
brevity
condense
density
elongate
emaciated
intend
meager
prolong

UNIT 18
aerate
aerial
airy
aspire
deflate
expire
hyperventilate
inflate
spirited
ventilate

UNIT 19
denounce
discount
fabled
fabulous
mythical
mythology
narrate
narrative
pronounce
recount

UNIT 20
ascertain
certainty
certify
concerted
conscience
ideal
idealistic
idealize
savor
savvy
scientific

UNIT ONE

FAC, FIC, FECT
Latin FACERE, FACTUM, "to make, do"

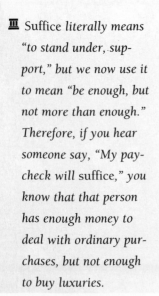

Be on the lookout for words with "fic," "fect," and "fy," as well as "fac" and "fact." All of these come from facere *and mean "making" or "doing."*

FACSIMILE (fak sim´ ə lē) *n.* A copy; an imitation
L. facere + similis, "like" = *made like*
That edition of the U.S. Constitution was a poor *facsimile* that looked like it was made on a cheap copier.
syn: duplicate

DEFICIENT (dē fish´ ənt) *adj.* Not having enough; lacking
L. de, "down," + facere = *made down, made less*
Mom wouldn't let us buy the cereal because she said it was *deficient* in vitamins.
syn: skimpy

You may have heard of petrified *wood. The word* petrify *can simply mean "to turn to stone"; this is what can happen to living material, like wood, over thousands of years. When we use* petrify *to mean "to scare," we are saying that someone is so frightened that he or she cannot move and seems to be made of stone.*

PETRIFY (pet´ rə fī) *v.* To scare; to frighten
L. petra, "stone," + facere = *to make stone*
The vampire movie *petrified* everyone in the theater so much that they were afraid to leave their seats.
syn: terrify   *ant:* comfort

AFFECTION (a fek´ shən) *n.* A feeling of love or liking; Tender feeling
L. ad, "towards," + facere = *to do towards*
Because Mary had a great deal of *affection* for Frank, she bought him a lovely farewell gift.
syn: tenderness   *ant:* disgust

SUFFICE (sə fīs´) *v.* To be enough
L. sub, "beneath, under" + facere = *to make or be under, support*
Betty didn't need any more friends; she felt that the ones she had would *suffice.*
syn: satisfy   *ant:* fall short

Suffice literally means "to stand under, support," but we now use it to mean "be enough, but not more than enough." Therefore, if you hear someone say, "My paycheck will suffice," you know that that person has enough money to deal with ordinary purchases, but not enough to buy luxuries.

I'd rather skate on ICE, but tile will SUFFICE.

ACT, AG
Latin AGERE, ACTUM, "to do, drive"

TRANSACT (trân zakt´) *v.* To carry out
L. trans, "across," + actum = *drive across*
The supermarket was closed, so Carrie couldn't *transact* any business there today.
syn: conduct

AGENDA (a jen´ də) *n.* A list of things to do
L. agenda, literally, "those things which must be done"
Dimitri said that the meeting's *agenda* included a report on income and one on spending.
syn: plan

COAGULATE (kō ag´ ū lāt) *v.* To solidify; to clump or clot
L. co, "together," + agere = *to drive together*
The snake kills its prey by injecting venom that makes its victim's blood *coagulate*.
syn: thicken   *ant*: thin

OPER
Latin OPERARE, OPERATUM, "to work"

INOPERABLE (in op´ ər ə bəl) *adj.*   1. Not working
                                              2. Not able to be fixed or cured
L. in, "not," + operare = *not able to work*
1. Someone jammed something in the lock yesterday, making it *inoperable*.
2. The kitten's owner was relieved to learn that her pet's disease was not *inoperable*.

COOPERATE (kō op´ ər āt) *v.* To work with; to be helpful to
L. co, "together," + operare = *to work together*
To win the final football game, all team members had to *cooperate* with one another.
syn: assist   *ant*: hinder

OPERATIONAL (op er ā´ shən əl) *adj.* In working order
The scientists found one minor problem in the robot, but most of the parts were still *operational*.

FUNCT
Latin FUNGI, FUNCTUM, "to work, to perform"

DEFUNCT (dē funkt´) *adj.* No longer working; no longer active
L. de, "down from," + "functum" = *down from work, no longer working*
The phone number I tried didn't work because the business was *defunct*.
syn: inactive   *ant*: working

MALFUNCTION (mal funk´ shən) *n.* Something that goes wrong; problem
L. male, "badly," + functum = *working badly*
Theresa was the one who discovered the *malfunction* that made the computer stop.
syn: error

III Coagulate *describes what some liquids or soft solids do over time, either with heat or because of a chemical reaction. Can you think of some liquids that coagulate?*

EXERCISES - UNIT ONE

Exercise I. Complete the sentence in a way that shows you understand the meaning of the italicized vocabulary word.

1. When doctors discovered that Daniel's tumor was *inoperable*, they…

2. The children were *petrified* by the shadow in the corner because…

3. Todd's *affection* for Lisa showed that their relationship was…

4. A *malfunction* in the jet engine forced the pilot to…

5. Terence's landscaping business is *defunct* because…

6. If the bank chooses to *transact* its business overseas, then…

7. The chemical that had spilled took only a short time to *coagulate*, so…

8. Robert's *agenda* for the camping trip included…

9. A cup of sugar did not *suffice* for the recipe because…

10. Because the bank robber would not *cooperate* with police…

11. It took a long time for the mill to become fully *operational* because…

12. Billy does not eat enough vegetables, so he is *deficient* in…

13. We knew that the document was a *facsimile* of the original contract rather than…

Exercise II. Fill in the blank with the best word from the choices below. One word will not be used.

deficient   facsimile   inoperable   transact   malfunction

1. The soil of the mountain town was _____ in certain nutrients that plants need in order to grow.

2. Tony was such a hard-working employee that he tried to _____ a sale even when he was on vacation.

3. Luckily, the _____ in my computer did not do any long-term damage.

4. If you cannot find your original driver's license, you can have a(n) _____ made.

Fill in the blank with the best word from the choices below. One word will not be used.

cooperate   suffice   petrifies   coagulates   defunct

5.   Will the number of classes you have taken _____, or will you have to take one more?

6.   The idea of giving a speech to a large group _____ Toby, so he never volunteers to do presentations.

7.   Once the milk _____, you will have a solid substance that will look like cheese.

8.   Because the woman pulled over for speeding would not _____ with police, she was arrested.

Fill in the blank with the best word from the choices below. One word will not be used.

transact   agenda   operational   defunct   inoperable   affection

9.   The new surgery brought hope to people who had been told their problems were _____.

10.   Unless we have a firm _____ for the meeting, we will not know what topics need to be covered.

11.   After the power outage, the police station's computer network was not _____.

12.   We were surprised when the _____ car that had been sitting in the driveway suddenly started.

13.   My puppies often showed their _____ for me by coming to sit on my lap.

Exercise III. Choose the set of words that best completes the sentence.

1.   Because Jordan is _____ in a particular vitamin, his blood will not _____.
      A.   inoperable; suffice
      B.   deficient; coagulate
      C.   operational; transact
      D.   deficient; petrify

2.   The booming thunder had _____ the horses; they would not _____ with the rancher.
      A.   petrified; cooperate
      B.   coagulated; malfunction
      C.   transacted; suffice
      D.   cooperated; transact

3.   Even though the teacher felt great _____ for her student, she told him that his short report would not _____.
      A.   agenda; malfunction
      B.   affection; suffice
      C.   facsimile; transact
      D.   affection; cooperate

4.   When the bank is fully _____, its employees will be able to _____ business from any-
     where in the world.
     A. deficient; transact
     B. inoperable; suffice
     C. defunct; petrify
     D. operational; transact

5.   We had many places listed on our travel _____, but a(n) _____ in our car's engine
     kept us from getting to them.
     A. agenda; malfunction
     B. facsimile; agenda
     C. affection; malfunction
     D. malfunction; agenda

Exercise IV. Complete the sentence by inferring information about the italicized word from its context.

1.   The thing that *petrified* us the most during the nature presentation was...

2.   When there is a *malfunction* in the car, the owner should ...

3.   If the half-hour meeting lasts two hours, it probably means the *agenda*...

**Exercise V. Fill in the blank with the word from the Unit that best completes the sentence, using the root
     we supply as a clue. Then, answer the questions that follow the paragraphs.**

All societies have some form of government. From the earliest times, social groups have recognized the need for some people to make and enforce decisions about the individual behavior that affects society in general. The encouraged behavior helps society run smoothly. For example, traffic rules and regulations help keep the roadways in working order. Most people willingly _____ (OPER) with these rules and regulations because they recognize the benefit not only to others but also to themselves.

In order for a government to work, citizens must accept that it belongs in power. People in a democratic society, such as the United States, have the benefit of electing government officials. In this way, the government is given authority by the governed people themselves. This, of course, is very different from the idea that God gives one ruler supreme control over all people. In some countries other than the United States, the king or queen has this kind of complete power.

From an early age, citizens are taught to obey the government. This teaching process, which takes place in the schools, for example, encourages people to accept the rules of society and to feel loyalty to symbols of the government such as the flag or national anthem.

Government also cares a lot about *jurisdiction*, which is the geographic area within which its laws are in effect. People may escape a government's jurisdiction only by moving to another country. In addition, government concerns itself with certain areas of people's individual lives. The government may make laws about national defense, social welfare, the economy, marriage and divorce, health, education, taxes, and transportation.

Law enforcement is also something taken care of by the government. Though for most people, the rules that are in place will _____ (FIC), others may need some kind of outside persuasion, such as the threat of punishment, before they will obey the law. Agents of the law, such as police officers, judges, and soldiers, work on society's behalf to make sure the laws are followed.

In diverse societies like the United States, representatives of special-interest groups—business, farming, labor, racial or ethnic, for instance—work with national or local governments to develop policies which will be good for the general public. This way, all elements of society are represented in government, and no one group can easily overpower another.

1.   The author defines government as
     A.   a group of people who make and enforce decisions affecting society.
     B.   elected politicians.
     C.   the U. S. Congress.
     D.   people who make rules.

2.   Why are special-interest groups important to a diverse society?
     A.   They ensure that all aspects of society are represented by government decisions.
     B.   They encourage favoritism.
     C.   They help the government pass laws.
     D.   They encourage people to obey laws.

3.   What role does jurisdiction play in government's rule?
     A.   It defines the area where the government is allowed to act.
     B.   It helps criminals escape.
     C.   People often relocate to escape arrest.
     D.   Jurisdiction adds to the government's power.

4.   Which of the following is a distinguishing feature of a democratic government?
     A.   Citizens always like the President.
     B.   Citizens have the right to election, through which they grant authority to officials.
     C.   The king has no power to rule.
     D.   All laws are fair.

5.   What is the best title for this article?
     A.   Constitutional Law
     B.   U. S. Law
     C.   Law Enforcement
     D.   Law and Government

**Exercise VI. Drawing on your knowledge of roots and words in context, read the following selection and
     define the *italicized* words. If you cannot figure out the meaning of the words on your own, look them
     up in a dictionary. Note that *bene* means "good."**

The bag Sharon just bought is *functional* as well as beautiful. It can be used for so many things because it
has lots of space for larger items, as well as pockets of different sizes for storing small objects like pencils and
pens, lip balm, and stamps. Her recent purchase of the bag is *beneficial* to her kids, too; their medicine, small
toys, and candy can be stored in a special compartment of the bag.

UNIT TWO

POS, PON
Latin PONERE, POSITUM "to put, place"

DEPOSIT   (dē poz´ ət)   *v.*   To put down; to drop
L. de, "down," + positum = *put down*
The cab driver did not wish to *deposit* his passengers in the middle of the dangerous street, so he drove to the side of the road.
syn: deliver   *ant*: pick up

COMPOSITION   (kom pə zi´ shən)   *n.*   The makeup of something
L. com, "together," + positum = *put together*
syn: content

PROPOSITION   (prop ə zi´ shən)   *n.*   An idea put forth; a suggestion
L. pro, "forth," + positum = *put forth*
The President made a *proposition* to Congress to provide money to rebuild the nation's electric system.
syn: offer

OPPONENT   (ə pō´ nənt)   *n.*   One who goes against; rival
L. ob, "opposite, in the way of," + positum = *put opposite*
One by one, Darryl's *opponents* in the marathon race fell farther behind him.
syn: competitor   *ant*: ally

MAN
Latin MANERE, MANSUM, "stay, remain"

IMPERMANENT   (im pûr´ mən ənt)   *adj.*   Not lasting forever
L. in, "not," + per, "throughout," + manere = *not lasting throughout*
Few relationships last forever; most of them are *impermanent*.
syn: passing   *ant*: eternal

REMNANT   (rem´ nənt)   *n.*   Something left over
L. re, "back," + manere = *to stay back*
The only *remnant* of the building that Sgt. Osbourn could find after the fire was a badly burned door.
syn: remainder

Sidebar notes:

▥ *The noun* deposit *means "something put down," whether it is money in a bank or sediment on the bottom of a river.*

▥ *A* composition *is also anything arranged by an artist, musician or author.*

STAT, STAN
Latin STARE, STATUM, "to stand, stay"

STATUS   (sta´ təs)   *n.*   A condition or situation
Can you tell me the *status* of my application?
syn: position

CIRCUMSTANCE   (sûr´ kəm stâns)   *n.* Condition surrounding something; a
        situation
L. circum, "around," + statum = *(events) standing around*
The police wondered what kind of *circumstance* would make a man try to break
into a jail.

CONSTANT   (kon´ stənt)   *n.*   Something that stays the same
L. con, intensifier, + statum = *standing*
Vince felt that the only *constant* in his life was Thunder, his faithful dog.

STATIONARY   (stā´ shən ər ē)   *adj.*   Standing still; not moving
Mark preferred the thrill of the open road to his *stationary* bicycle.
syn: stable   *ant:* traveling; moveable

The paper blew away, but the desk STAYED STATIONARY.

III *Remember that some prefixes can mean "very" or "completely." A constant is something that not only stands, but stands through everything; it does not change.*

EXERCISES - UNIT TWO

Exercise I. Complete the sentence in a way that shows you understand the meaning of the italicized vocabulary word.

1. When I made my opening statement, my *opponent* on the debate team…

2. Serita's *proposition* about going out for dinner was rejected because…

3. One *circumstance* that might cause the picnic to be cancelled is…

4. Scientists wondered if the strange piece of metal was a *remnant* of the satellite because…

5. In order to check the *status* of the departing flight, Patricia…

6. Geologists studied the *composition* of the mysterious rock because…

7. We wanted to *deposit* all the Halloween candy…

8. Because snow is a *constant* in the Brownsville weather forecast…

9. We learned how *impermanent* sand castles could be when…

10. The police ordered the suspect to remain *stationary* because…

Exercise II. Fill in the blank with the best word from the choices below. One word will not be used.

compositions　　opponents　　remnant　　constant　　stationary

1. The storm system is currently _____ and will probably not move for several more days.

2. A(n) _____ of the sunken ship could be seen sticking out from the water.

3. Although Vicki and Ray had always been friends, they became _____ when they stepped onto the basketball court.

4. The economy seems to change all the time; it is difficult to find any kind of _____ in it.

Fill in the blank with the best word from the choices below. One word will not be used.

circumstances   status   impermanent   composition

5.   Latitia was told that her best friend's _____ at the hospital had not changed.

6.   Although various kinds of pollution are dumped into the ocean each year, its _____ remains basically the same.

7.   When we thought about the _____ that had caused our financial problems, we realized what we should have done.

Fill in the blank with the best word from the choices below. One word will not be used.

deposited   proposition   impermanent   composition

8.   The students in the cafeteria could not have breakfast until the truck _____ their daily supply of milk.

9.   Allie's bad mood was a(n) _____ part of her character, and it quickly changed to cheerfulness.

10. The President rejected the Senator's _____ to ban parking on downtown streets.

Exercise III. Choose the set of words that best completes the sentence.

1.   The _____ of the soil in our backyard is _____; it changes depending on the weather and the time of year.
     A.   proposition; constant
     B.   composition; impermanent
     C.   opponent; stationary
     D.   circumstance; constant

2.   Trent asked about the _____ of the budget, then made a(n) _____ that he thought would save the City Council money.
     A.   status; proposition
     B.   circumstance; opponent
     C.   deposit; proposition
     D.   constant; status

3.   The 375-pound fighter was able to pick up his _____ and _____ the poor man in the other corner of the ring.
     A.   composition; deposit
     B.   remnant; proposition
     C.   circumstance; deposit
     D.   opponent; deposit

4. In the machine, there are many moving parts that frequently change position; the only _____ is the center rod, which is always _____.
   A. circumstance; impermanent
   B. constant; stationary
   C. status; constant
   D. remnant; impermanent

5. Through a lucky _____, the missing _____ of the original sculpture was discovered in someone's attic.
   A. circumstance; remnant
   B. constant; opponent
   C. composition; status
   D. proposition; opponent

Exercise IV. Complete the sentence by inferring information about the italicized word from its context.

1. You might need to know the *status* of your application if…

2. The tiger remained quiet and *stationary* because it…

3. If police find *remnants* of explosives in the destroyed building, it probably means…

Exercise V. Fill in the blank with the word from the Unit that best completes the sentence, using the root we supply as a clue. Then, answer the questions that follow the paragraphs.

Today, the United States has a central banking system. In this system, a central bank is linked to many smaller ones. Countries throughout the world operate the same systems as a way of controlling their money. The United States' central banking system is called the Federal Reserve. Although this exists in the United States today, however, it has not always been part of our country's economic structure.

In 1791, George Washington set up the first central bank in the United States. It was called the First Bank of the United States. There were controversies surrounding it, but it was generally considered to be a success. Thomas Jefferson was a(n) _____ (PON) of the Bank of the United States because it gave the government too much power. The First Bank of the United States closed in 1811 because of _____ (STAN) related to these suspicions.

State institutions were responsible for the country's money after that time; the _____ (STAT) of the national economy was uncertain until the rise of another central bank. This came about in 1816, when the Second Bank of the United States was opened. Eventually it, too, closed, forcing the US to return to state banks for services. From 1837 to 1863, the national government did not control the banking system. This period is known as the Free Banking Era.

There were further attempts to improve the banking system. With the National Banking Acts of 1863 and 1864, the government sought to control the nation's finances, but without a central bank.

Eventually, in 1913, the Federal Reserve System was set up. Of course, the Federal Reserve System has not remained the same since it was first developed. For example, the Depression of 1929 caused people to panic, and many banks closed. As a result, when President Roosevelt was elected in 1932, he passed laws to make the financial program safer. An increase in the use of technology has also affected the way our money moves. Our country has gone through many changes since the opening of the First Bank of the United States.

1.   Which of the following sentences is true, according to the article?
      A.   The National Banking Acts were set up in 1863 and 1864.
      B.   The United States is the only country in the world with a central banking system.
      C.   The Aldrich Plan was written in 1920.
      D.   The Depression had no effect on the banking system in the United States.

2.   The central banking system in the United States today is called the
      A.   Bank of the United States.
      B.   United States Federal Reserve.
      C.   National Banking System.
      D.   Federal Bank of the United States.

3.   Which of the following sentences is NOT true about the central banking system in the United States?
      A.   The United States government has control over the central banking system.
      B.   The United States' central bank is linked to smaller banks.
      C.   The banking system in the United States has gone through many changes.
      D.   The United States has always had a central banking system.

4.   The best title for this passage would be
      A.   "Banks Throughout the World."
      B.   "The History of Central Banking in the United States."
      C.   "Banking Problems."
      D.   "State Banks and the United States."

Exercise VI. Drawing on your knowledge of roots and words in context, read the following selection and define the *italicized* words. If you cannot figure out the meaning of the words on your own, look them up in a dictionary. Note that *im* means "on."

When Governor Jarlsberg tried to *impose* new taxes on the city, the people living here decided they were not going to take it. Taxes were already at an all-time high; more taxes on top of these would lead to economic disaster. There were riots in the streets downtown; people marched around with signs that read, "Down with Jarlsberg's taxes!" The governor decided to *station* police at major intersections so that they could stop any destruction before it got out of hand.

UNIT THREE

CAP, CAPT, CIP
Latin CAPERE, CAPTUM, "to seize, take, get"

CAPACITY   (kə pas´ ə tē)   *n.*   An ability; potential
Dave didn't have the *capacity* to forgive his sister after all the teasing she put him through.
syn: power   *ant:* inability

CAPTIVATE   (kap´ tə vāt)   *v.*   To interest greatly; to charm
Cute puppies *captivated* the artist so much that they were the only thing he ever painted.
syn: fascinate   *ant:* bore

RECIPIENT   (rē sip´ ē ənt)   *n.*   A person who gets something
L. re, "back," + capere = *get back*
Elizabeth was thrilled to be the *recipient* of the front-row ticket to the show.

PREHEND
Latin PREHENDERE, PREHENSUM, "to seize, to grasp, to take"

APPREHEND   (ap rē hend´)   *v.*   To seize; to arrest
L. ad, "upon," + prehendere = *to seize upon*
The escaped bank robber was quickly *apprehended* when he tried to steal a police car.
syn: capture   *ant:* release

COMPREHEND   (kom prē hend´)   *v.*   To understand
L. com, "with," + prehendere = *to seize with* (the mind)
No matter how much he studied, Mel could not *comprehend* any foreign language.
syn: get, grasp   *ant:* mistake

▥ *Note: Now that you know "fic" (from Unit 1) is just another form of "fac," it will be easy to remember that "cip" is another form of "cap."*

▥ *To* apprehend *is "to catch or seize"; if you feel* apprehensive, *you are seized by doubt or worry about something yet to come.*

SUM, SUMPT
Latin SUMERE, SUMPTUM, "take, use up, buy"

ASSUMPTION (ə sump´ shən) *n.* A belief accepted as true
L. ad, "to," + sumere = *to take towards (oneself)*
Ed made the false *assumption* that he could outrun his father in a long race.

CONSUME (kən sōōm´) *v.* To use up; devour
L. con, intensifier, + sumere = *to completely use up*
How could the Smiths *consume* so much electricity when their air conditioner never runs?
syn: go through   *ant*: save

PRESUMPTUOUS (prē zump´ chōō əs) *adj.* Having too much confidence
L. pre, "before," + sumptum = *to take in advance*
It was *presumptuous* of Gary to think I was his friend simply because I agreed with him about the movie.
syn: forward   *ant*: humble

SUMPTUOUS (sump´ chōō əs) *adj.* Very luxurious or rich
Ted thought the meal of steak and lobster was *sumptuous*, but his date felt it was overly fancy and cost too much.
syn: magnificent   *ant*: plain

SOME CHEW the SUMPTUOUS food with eyes closed.

RAPT, RAP
Latin RAPERE, RAPTUM, "to seize"

RAPTURE (rapt´ shər) *n.* A state of intense joy
Few things compare to the *rapture* little Emily feels when her father holds her closely.
syn: bliss   *ant*: misery

RAPIDITY (ra pid´ i tē) *n.* Speed; quickness
Sally had no trouble understanding the teacher, even though he went through the lessons with great *rapidity*.
syn: hurry   *ant*: slowness

▥ *To* assume *is to take something for granted; it can also mean "to put on or take up." If the captain of your volleyball team is hurt, you can* assume *that he or she will get better, but you can also* assume *the role of captain in the meantime.*

▥ *If you are* presumptuous, *you believe you have the right to do something when you actually do not have the right. It would be* presumptuous *of you to decide on a movie without asking your friends what they wanted to see.*

▥ *The Latin verb "sumere" means both "to take" and "to buy, spend money on." Something* sumptuous *usually takes a great deal of money to purchase.*

EXERCISES - UNIT THREE

Exercise I. Complete the sentence in a way that shows you understand the meaning of the italicized vocabulary word.

1.   Once teachers had *apprehended* the fleeing student, they...

2.   Darren was the *recipient* of several awards for his architecture because...

3.   The actress has *captivated* audiences across America because...

4.   The *assumption* that George will not visit the dentist is wrong because...

5.   Linda was not able to *comprehend* what had happened to her car until...

6.   Cynthia felt *rapture* as she stood on the tropical beach because...

7.   Because Hal's office has a large, fast computer network, he has the *capacity* to...

8.   When we entered the dining room and saw the *sumptuous* meal, we...

9.   In response to her sister's rather *presumptuous* question, Carla...

10. When the cows have *consumed* all the grass in the pasture, they will...

11. Charles finished his morning chores with great *rapidity* because...

Exercise II. Fill in the blank with the best word from the choices below. One word will not be used.

assumption   rapture   rapidity   capacity   recipient

1.   The _____ with which Dottie ate surprised her father because she had once been a very slow eater.

2.   Trent was surprised when the _____ of the gift decided to return it.

3.   Because the washing machine did not have the _____ to handle so many loads, it quickly broke down.

4.   You make the _____ that I ate the cake, but how can you be sure?

Fill in the blank with the best word from the choices below. One word will not be used.

captivated   sumptuous   rapture   consumed   presumptuous

5.   The king was wearing _____ silks and linens, which were wonderful to touch.

6.   Some of the children loved the carousel, while others felt _____ at the sight of the Ferris wheel.

7.   As a child, Lawrence was _____ by the sights and sounds of the market.

8.   Scooter felt that it would be _____ of him to enter his neighbor's house without being invited.

Fill in the blank with the best word from the choices below. One word will not be used.

capacity   apprehend   consumes   comprehend

9.   Katerina cannot _____ why anyone would want to spend a Saturday evening at home.

10.   Once a python _____ a small animal, it will not need to eat again for several weeks.

11.   In an effort to _____ men wanted by the police, the government began searching local neighborhoods.

Exercise III. Choose the set of words that best completes the sentence.

1.   Tim's story of the _____ gifts laid out at the wedding banquet _____ all of us.
    A. presumptuous; apprehended
    B. sumptuous; comprehended
    C. sumptuous; captivated
    D. captivating; apprehended

2.   Do not make the _____ that Ralph is a snob simply because he has been the _____ of so many awards.
    A. recipient; rapture
    B. rapture; capacity
    C. rapidity; assumption
    D. assumption; recipient

3.   Although small children have the _____ to lie, they cannot _____ the difference between right and wrong.
    A. rapidity; apprehend
    B. capacity; comprehend
    C. assumption; consume
    D. rapture; captivate

4.   The two policemen set off with _____ in order to _____ the suspect.
     A.   recipient; captivate
     B.   rapture; comprehend
     C.   rapidity; apprehend
     D.   recipient; consume

5.   Gretel felt _____ at the sight of the candy store and wished she could _____ all the candy at once.
     A.   rapture; consume
     B.   rapidity; comprehend
     C.   recipient; captivate
     D.   capacity; apprehend

Exercise IV. Complete the sentence by inferring information about the italicized word from its context.

1.   Someone who is the *recipient* of a million dollars should feel...

2.   If Stacie prepares a *sumptuous* meal, her family will probably...

3.   When the river moves with much *rapidity*, you should most likely...

Exercise V. Fill in the blank with the word from the Unit that best completes the sentence, using the root we supply as a clue. Then, answer the questions that follow the paragraphs.

It is often said that prisons make prisoners worse. Some people make the _____ (SUMPT) that the prison environment, one of drugs and violence, actually makes a criminal immune to positive change. When prisoners return to society, say these people, they renew a negative cycle of criminal activity, arrest, and punishment. However, there is also evidence that a good prison program can produce positive results, turning a prisoner into a productive member of society.

What are the signs of a good prison program? Psychologists who have studied this issue have focused on several important principles that must be present in any successful program. First, it must address all the needs of the prisoner. For example, it is not enough to help someone get off drugs if he or she doesn't know how to read. Likewise, it is not enough to help a prisoner read if he or she cannot communicate with others or _____ (PREHEND) how others feel. All concerns, including substance abuse, education, and future employment, must be addressed. Second, not all prisoners should receive the same treatment. Although it is not an easy thing to do, prison psychologists must try to determine which prisoners are more likely to offend again and give them more intensive treatment than they give the others. Third, programs must be responsive to the prisoner's ability to participate in the programs. Some prisoners are willing and more able to be _____

(CIP) of aid programs than others are. Those having difficulty participating may need extra help, so that they, too, can begin to benefit from the programs available to them. Finally, the programs must be managed by well-trained staff and must last long enough to be worthwhile.

Of course, even with the best programs, there will still be some prisoners who are unable to be reformed. The failure rate, however, is small. Given a good program, only about one-quarter of prisoners will commit crimes again. In a poor program, almost three-quarters of the prisoners will reenter a life of crime. A good prison program, therefore, is of great value to society. It is important that taxpayers accept the cost of helping the prisoners reform because, in the long run, it is less costly than having more crime on the streets. For example, a recent study by the White House Office of National Drug Control found that while a specific treatment might cost approximately three thousand dollars, the benefit to society was over nine thousand dollars. In other words, good programs are worth the cost.

If the principles outlined above are applied to prison programs in our country, good results are bound to occur. The value of prisons, then, will not be that they keep bad people locked away from good people, but rather that they help prisoners who have done bad things learn to become productive members of society.

1.   Which sentence below best sums up a main idea of the passage?
      A. Prisons only make prisoners worse.
      B. Good prison programs can produce good results.
      C. Prisons keep bad people locked away from good people.
      D. Good prison programs make sure all their prisoners will not commit crimes again.

2.   This article states that taxpayers should accept the cost of helping prisoners reform because
      A. society owes it to them.
      B. prisoners expect to be helped.
      C. good programs are less costly than more crime on the streets.
      D. all of the above

3.   A study mentioned in the article found that
      A. a good treatment program in prison might cost nine thousand dollars.
      B. society saves three thousand dollars with every good treatment for prisoners.
      C. good treatment programs might be costly, but they are well worth it.
      D. None of the above

4.   Psychologists have found that
      A. not all prisoners should be treated alike.
      B. all prisoners should be treated alike.
      C. prisoners who are not treated alike are resentful.
      D. prisoners who are not treated alike are more likely to commit crime again.

Exercise VI. Drawing on your knowledge of roots and words in context, read the following selection and define the *italicized* words. If you cannot figure out the meaning of the words on your own, look them up in a dictionary. Note that *anti* means "before" and *re* means "again."

The football game has stopped for now because of dangerous thunder and lightning. The men and women in the stands *anticipate* that it will start again within half an hour. They expect this because the storm is moving quickly and should be over soon. If the game does *resume* within a short time, we will be able to watch it until the end and still get home in time for dinner.

UNIT FOUR

REG, REIG
Latin REX, REGIS, "king"

REGAL   (rē´ gəl)   *adj.*   Of or like a king or queen
Keith's *regal* costume for Halloween even included a cape and crown.
syn: royal

REIGN   (rān)   *n.*   Authority; rule
The new queen caught a deadly disease, so her *reign* lasted only a month.
syn: power   *ant*: servitude

REGICIDE   (rej´ ə sīd)   *n.*   The murder of a king
L. regis + caedere, "to kill" = *killing of a king*
King John's son committed *regicide* to take over the country; he also killed his mother.

VICT
Latin VINCERE, VICTUM, "to conquer"

CONVICT   (kən vikt´)   *v.*   To find guilty
L. con, "completely," + victum = *completely conquer*
Despite the evidence against him, Herman wouldn't admit that he committed the crime; the jury *convicted* him anyway.
                              ant: acquit

VICTORIOUS   (vik tor´ ē əs)   *adj.*   Winning or succeeding
Helen was proud that she was *victorious* in the statewide spelling bee.
syn: successful   *ant*: losing

EVICT   (ē vikt´)   *v.*   To force to leave
L. e, "completely," + victum = *completely conquer, force out*
An aggressive intruder *evicted* the smaller birds from the nest.
syn: chase out   *ant*: welcome

Regalia once meant "the symbols and accessories of royalty"; we now use the word to refer to the decorations of any important person or group.

The noun convict means "someone who has been found guilty of a crime." or "felon."

POSS, POT
Latin POTENS, "powerful"
POSSE, "to be able"

POSSESSIVE (pə zes´ iv) *adj.* Wanting to own or control; jealous
Maria was very *possessive* of her toys and wouldn't let her little sister play with them.

POTENT (pō´ tənt) *adj.* Very strong or powerful
The tiny snake's venom was quick and *potent*; it could kill a person in less than ten minutes.

ant: weak

OMNIPOTENT (om nip´ ə tənt) *adj.* Ruling all; all-powerful
L. omnis, "all," + potens = *all-powerful*
King Charles I believed he was *omnipotent*, but he was overthrown and executed.

syn: almighty

DOM
Latin DOMINARI, DOMINATUM, "to rule"
DOMUS, "house"

DOMESTIC (də mes´ tik) *adj.* Having to do with the home
Harold felt that *domestic* tasks like dishwashing were beneath him.

DOMINATE (dom´ ə nāt) *v.* To rule completely
Our cheerleading team has *dominated* the annual tournament for three years.
syn: command   *ant*: serve

DOMINION (də min´ yən) *n.* An area ruled or controlled
The *dominion* of the last Russian Czars was enormous, covering millions of square miles.
syn: territory

DOMICILE (dōm´ ə sīl) *n.* A home
When the divorced parents decided to stay in the same *domicile*, their kids were extremely happy.
syn: abode

Our backyard pond became the DOMICILE of a CROCODILE.

▥ Domino *also comes from* DOMINARI. *How do you think these words are related?*

▥ *The Latin word* DOMUS *means "house." The Latin noun* DOMINUS *means "master of the house." The verb* DOMINARI *comes from* DOMINUS, *and has to do with being master, ruling, and power.*

EXERCISES - UNIT FOUR

Exercise I. Complete the sentence in a way that shows you understand the meaning of the italicized vocabulary word.

1.   Shawn's basketball team was *victorious* today, so Shawn…

2.   The *reign* of Peter as yearbook editor was brought to an end by…

3.   The country was stunned by news of the *regicide* because…

4.   In order to *dominate* the other baseball teams in our league, we will have to…

5.   The drug I was given when I had the flu was so *potent* that…

6.   During the nineteenth century, because many women were allowed only *domestic* jobs…

7.   The jury decides today whether it will *convict* the accused woman or…

8.   The villagers no longer wished to be under the *dominion* of the Queen because…

9.   The landlord says that he will be forced to *evict* us if we do not…

10.   Walter was very *possessive* when it came to his new friend because…

11.   I always thought my mother was *regal* in appearance because she…

12.   The store manager considered himself *omnipotent*, but was actually…

13.   Jesse was happiest in his *domicile* because…

Exercise II. Fill in the blank with the best word from the choices below. One word will not be used.

   regal   domestic   possessive   victorious   reign

1.   Carson quit his job for a more _____ lifestyle because he wanted to take better care of his house and children.

2.   The dictator's _____ of terror lasted until a new ruler came into power.

3.   If Cherie does not practice carefully, she will not be _____ in the French competition.

4.   There is no need to be _____ about your ice-cream cone, since no one is going to take it.

Fill in the blank with the best word from the choices below. One word will not be used.

> dominion   regal   potent   convicted   omnipotent

5.   Looking to expand her _____, the queen sent her army to invade the neighboring territory.

6.   Dressed in his _____robes, the king stood before his people.

7.   Katie was not _____ of the crime because she produced new evidence at the last minute.

8.   In the kindergarten classroom, the teacher seems _____; she controls everything that happens during the day.

Fill in the blank with the best word from the choices below. One word will not be used.

> possessive   dominate   potent   evicted   regicide   domicile

9.   When the large business bought the small company, it _____ several employees from the office.

10.   Often, the stronger dogs in the pack will try to _____ the weaker ones.

11.   I cleaned the bathroom with a chemical so _____ it could strip paint off the walls.

12.   The prince threatened _____ if his father did not give up the throne.

13.   My mother's desk at work was messy, but she kept her _____ spotless.

Exercise III. Choose the set of words that best completes the sentence.

1.   King Solomon believed that his _____ jewels had magical powers that made him _____ and allowed him to rule over the whole world.
    A.   domestic; regal
    B.   omnipotent; possessive
    C.   victorious; regal
    D.   regal; omnipotent

2.   If the governor is _____ in the upcoming election, she will _____ over the state for seven years.
    A.   possessive; evict
    B.   victorious; reign
    C.   potent; convict
    D.   regal; convict

3.   The princess wishes rule over her father's _____, but would never commit _____ to gain it.
    A.   dominion; regicide
    B.   domicile; reign
    C.   regicide; dominion
    D.   reign; victorious

4.   My roommate is very _____ about his things and has threatened to _____ me if I touch any of his stuff.
      A.   omnipotent; reign
      B.   regal; convict
      C.   potent; dominate
      D.   possessive; evict

5.   If the famous golfer is _____ of burning down the school, the story will surely _____ the newspapers for weeks.
      A.   evicted; convict
      B.   convicted; dominate
      C.   reigned; evict
      D.   dominated; reign

Exercise IV. Complete the sentence by inferring information about the italicized word from its context.

1.   If Kasey's *domicile* isn't large enough, she can always…

2.   The mayor is small and never yells, but she *dominates*…

3.   If Tiffany was *evicted* from her apartment, it probably means…

Exercise V. Fill in the blank with the word from the Unit that best completes the sentence, using the root we supply as a clue. Then, answer the questions that follow the paragraphs.

Americans have been raised to believe that monarchy is not an acceptable form of government, yet plenty of monarchies continue to flourish throughout the world. Sweden, Denmark, The Netherlands, and Norway are some modern kingdoms with kind and benevolent kings and queens. However, there was a time when Sweden wanted to rule the world, and a tyrannical ruler came to power. His reign only ended with his death.

Gustavus III was born in 1746, the eldest son of King Adolphus Frederick and Queen Lovisa Ulrika of Prussia. He received a classical education common among the nobility, then entered into an arranged and loveless marriage to a Danish princess, Sofia Magdalena, daughter of the King of Denmark. In 1771, while Gustavus was in France, he received the news that his father had died and that he had risen to the throne. A long-time admirer of the French and its more powerful dynasty, Gustavus sought to similarly _____(DOM) the nobility of his country and the Swedish Parliament, known as the Riksdag.

Gustavus gained control over the Riksdag, then dismantled it and made himself absolute ruler over foreign and _____(DOM) affairs. The now-powerless nobles did not take their loss without complaint, and tensions only became worse over the next twenty years as Gustavus continually ignored them, raised their taxes, and threatened to repossess their estates should they defy him.

With power secured at home, Gustavus tried to increase his _____ (DOM) over his neighbors, via a war against Denmark. Then, in 1787, he ordered troops into Russia, with disastrous results.

To_____ (VICT) Gustavus from the throne, the Swedish nobles saw no other choice but to murder him. After a formal ball at the Royal Opera House in Stockholm, on March 16, 1792, J. J. Anckarstöm committed _____ (REG) by shooting the King in the back during an unattended moment. Gustavus didn't die immediately, but suffered pain until his death on March 29th. He was forty-six years old.

1.   Gustavus III was born in what century?
      A. 16th
      B. 20th
      C. 18th
      D. 17th

2.   How did Gustavus III become king?
      A. He was elected.
      B. His father died.
      C. He led a revolution.
      D. The Riksdag appointed him.

3.   Sweden belongs to what geographic region?
      A. Asia
      B. Australia
      C. Balkans
      D. Scandinavia

4.   What country did Gustavus III wish to imitate?
      A. Germany
      B. France
      C. Italy
      D. Spain

5.   What is the Riksdag?
      A. a noble organization
      B. a German club
      C. Sweden's parliament
      D. Norway's parliament

Exercise VI. Drawing on your knowledge of roots and words in context, read the following selection and define the *italicized* words. If you cannot figure out the meaning of the words on your own, look them up in a dictionary.

The emperor wants to make his empire bigger for several reasons. The first is that a bigger country will be more powerful and able to defend itself when attacked by other nations. Second, he needs more money; new land will allow more crops to be sold and more gold and silver that can be mined. Finally, this *potentate* wants to spread his religion to as many people and places as he can. All of these are good reasons for him to try to expand his *domain*.

UNIT FIVE

JAC, JECT
Latin JACERE, JECTUM, "to throw, hurl"

ADJACENT (ə jā´ sənt) *adj.* Next to; nearby
L. ad, "towards," + jacere = *thrown towards*
Do you know the names of the states that are *adjacent* to your home state?
syn: neighboring   *ant:* distant

SUBJECT (sub jekt´) *v.* To cause to undergo or experience
L. sub, "beneath," + jectum = *thrown beneath*
Protesters were angry that the animal was *subjected* to cruelty as a way of testing
its reactions to various chemicals.
syn: expose   *ant:* protect

PROJECTILE (prō jek´ təl) *n.* Something sent through the air
L. pro, "forth," + jectum = *thrown forth*
The mechanical arm was able to throw the *projectile* much farther than I was.

BALL, BOL, BL
Greek BALLEIN, "to throw"

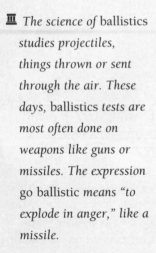

BALLISTIC (bə lis´ tik) *adj.* Thrown or projected
The bullet's *ballistic* properties were studied while it was in midair.

PARABLE (pa´ rə bəl) *n.* A story with a moral message or lesson
G. para, "beside," + ballein, "to throw" = *to throw beside*
Many stories are not exactly about what they seem to be; these are sometimes
known as *parables*.

SYMBOLIZE (sim´ bəl īz) *v.* To stand for; to represent
G. sym, "together," + ballein = *thrown together*
In primitive cultures, the sun often is used to
symbolize life and rebirth.
syn: signify

III The science of ballistics
studies projectiles,
*things thrown or sent
through the air. These
days,* ballistics *tests are
most often done on
weapons like guns or
missiles. The expression*
go ballistic *means "to
explode in anger," like a
missile.*

III A parable *is a story told
as another story or idea
for comparison. If the
first story is hard to
understand, a* parable
can help explain it.

*In this symphony, the sound of CYMBALS
SYMBOLIZES thunder.*

PASS

Latin PANDERE, PASSUM, "spread out"
PASSUS, "a step"

ENCOMPASS (en kom´ pəs)   *v.*   To include; to cover
Karen tried to *encompass* all her feelings for her mother in a short poem.
syn: contain   *ant:* leave out

PASSABLE (pas´ ə bəl)   *adj.*   Good enough, but not excellent
During his first year in Mexico, Darren's understanding of Spanish was barely
passable, but it improved rapidly after that.
syn: fair   *ant:* outstanding

PEND, PENS

Latin PENDERE, PENSUM, "to hang, to weigh"

APPENDIX (ə pen´ diks)   *n.*   Material added at the end of a book
L. ad, "upon," + pendere = *hang upon*
The biology textbook had only seven chapters, but it also contained a hundred-
page *appendix* that explained new discoveries.

DISPENSE (dis pens´)   *v.*   1. To give out; distribute
                    2. To get rid of
L. dis, "apart," + pensum = *to weigh out*
1. Medical personnel *dispensed* supplies to people who had been injured in the
   earthquake.
2. The museum robbers were forced to *dispense* of the stolen art as they ran from
   the police

SUSPEND (sə spend´)   *v.*   To stop; to put on hold
L. sub, "from beneath," + pendere = *to hang from beneath, hang up*
Marc *suspended* his search for a new car for the time being.
syn: shelve   *ant:* continue

▥ *The Latin word* passus
*means "a spreading out
of the foot, " or "step."
From this word we get
the words* pace, *com-
pass (including the
compass you may have
used in math class),*
encompass, *and* pass-
able, *along with many
other words.*

▥ *All people are born
with an* appendix, *an
organ in the body that
has no known function.*

EXERCISES - UNIT FIVE

Exercise I. Complete the sentence in a way that shows you understand the meaning of the italicized vocabulary word.

1.   The mill was forced to *suspend* its operations when…

2.   The soldiers raised the American flag to *symbolize*…

3.   Although Ben's performance in the math class was *passable*…

4.   The doctors will *subject* Jeremy to a variety of tests so that…

5.   When the children heard their mother's *parable*, they…

6.   In his book on the history of automobiles, the author tries to *encompass*…

7.   Because the grocery store was *adjacent* to a school…

8.   The reading teacher wanted the class to study the *appendix* to…

9.   The soda machine would not *dispense* cola because…

10.   When Daniel walked in front of the goal, a *projectile* similar to a soccer ball…

11.   The *ballistic* measurements of the slingshot showed that…

Exercise II. Fill in the blank with the best word from the choices below. One word will not be used.

adjacent   symbolize   projectile   parable   appendix

1.   My office was _____ to Eileen's, so I could hear every word of her phone conversations.

2.   To help the students explain why cheating is wrong, the teacher told them a(n) _____.

3.   The _____ that turned out to be a wet snowball hit the back of my head as I started for school.

4.   Tommy was the only person in class to know the answer; he had looked for it in the book's _____.

Fill in the blank with the best word from the choices below. One word will not be used.

subject   dispense   symbolize   suspend

5.   In this painting, flowers _____ hope and new life.

6.   "No matter what torture you _____ me to," cried the prisoner, "I will never give up my secret!"

7.   The referee said that unless the players stopped fighting, he would _____ the game.

Fill in the blank with the best word from the choices below. One word will not be used.

dispensed   subjected   encompass   ballistic   passable

8.   Darlene's acting in the play is _____, but could be much better.

9.   When dropped from great heights, an anvil can have as much force as (an) _____ missile.

10.   A freak snowstorm hit, but workers still _____ medicine in the town square.

11.   The weatherman's long-term forecast will _____ the six weeks between now and the end of the year.

Exercise III. Choose the set of words that best completes the sentence.

1.   The plans for new construction in the city _____ not only the area between 5th and Vine Street, but also the _____ vacant lot.
        A.   dispenses; ballistic
        B.   suspends; passable
        C.   encompass; adjacent
        D.   symbolizes; projectile

2.   Because James could not _____ himself to another boring lunch with Stan, he decided to eat whatever the candy machine would _____.
        A.   encompass; suspend
        B.   subject; dispense
        C.   symbolize; subject
        D.   dispense; encompass

3.   Scientists had to add a(n) _____ to their study of _____ when new information about wind resistance came out.
        A.   projectile; appendix
        B.   ballistic; parables
        C.   appendix; projectiles
        D.   passable; projectile

4.   Connie often uses _____ to explain what she means, and it's sometimes difficult to understand what the objects in these stories _____.
     A.   appendices; dispense
     B.   parables; suspend
     C.   projectiles; encompass
     D.   parables; symbolize

5.   If Steve's performance on his next driving test is not _____, the state may _____ his license.
     A.   ballistic; dispense
     B.   passable; suspend
     C.   projectile; encompass
     D.   passable; symbolize

Exercise IV. Complete the sentence by inferring information about the italicized word from its context.

1.   If your teacher tells you to consult the book's *appendix*, he probably wants you to…

2.   If Shawna is told that her essay is *passable*, she should feel…

3.   If Tom and his new wife move to the house *adjacent* to his old one, it may be because…

Exercise V. Fill in the blank with the word from the Unit that best completes the sentence, using the root we supply as a clue. Then, answer the questions that follow the paragraphs.

Teaching poetry is a difficult task. Many of us come to our first poetry lesson with the idea that poetry is something that simply "flows from the soul" like magic. It is important, therefore, for a teacher to point out that writing poetry is a craft that takes time. Poets carefully choose which words will go into their poems. They try different ones out, keep some, and reject others.

It is possible, though, to go too far with the idea that writing a poem is a precise and thoughtful task. Too often students come away thinking that all poems have "secret meanings" and that the job of the reader is to find those hidden meanings. "If a poem seems relatively straightforward," students are told, "you probably are not looking closely enough. Read the poem again and 'interpret' it."

For instance, look at William Carlos Williams' poem:

So much depends
upon
a red wheel
barrow
glazed with rain
water
beside the white
chickens.

For the most part, Williams was a poet who wrote about everyday things: plums, crunching leaves, a cat accidentally stepping into a flowerpot. He himself objected to the idea that the objects in this poem stood for other things.

A quick search on the Internet, though, shows that many readers have refused to take Williams at his word. Some insist that the poem is a _____ (BL) about the need to work hard: the wheelbarrow has faced the hardship of being rained upon, but it needs to rise above that because so much "depends" upon it; Williams "must" mean that people, too, should do this. Some believe that that red wheelbarrow, white chickens, and sad, or "blue" rain stand for the red, white, and blue of the American flag. Others say that the poem is about the Russian revolution and that the red wheelbarrow _____ (BOL) the blood of the worker while the rain water stands in for the workers' tears and sweat. One student, who admits that she was pressured to interpret the poem by her teacher, writes that Williams' chickens must be planning to sneak away from the farm and are depending upon the wheelbarrow for their escape. The rain, she writes, means that the chickens are planning to escape under cover of a storm. She goes on to comment that these must be highly organized chickens!

Although these interpreters probably mean well, they are so busy trying to puzzle out what they believe are Williams' secret intentions that they cannot focus on the most important part of the poem: its simplicity and clear language. If no one had ever forced them to believe that poems always mean something different from what they appear to, these readers could have appreciated Williams' poem for what it is: a simple picture of a simple scene on an ordinary day.

1.   In this passage, Williams' wheelbarrow is NOT compared to
      A. the red stripes on the American flag.
      B. the blood of the worker.
      C. the setting sun.
      D. the need to rise above hardship and work hard.

2.   Which statement would the author most likely agree with?
      A. William Carlos Williams did not write difficult poetry.
      B. Poetry should never be taught, just read.
      C. Not all poems have hidden meanings.
      D. No one would write a poem about chickens escaping from a farm.

3.   The author most likely thinks that Williams' poem is about
      A. a wheelbarrow and chickens.
      B. the joys of a simple life.
      C. what a wheelbarrow and chickens might symbolize.
      D. the fact that poetry is a craft.

Exercise VI. Drawing on your knowledge of roots and words in context, read the following selection and define the *italicized* words. If you cannot figure out the meaning of the words on your own, look them up in a dictionary. Note that *inter* means "between."

The dog's *pendulous* ears are the perfect addition to his funny face. They hang down several inches and flop around when he runs. Once, the dog's owner, Alexis, got into an argument with her brother George about whether one of the dog's ears was longer than the other. They went back and forth in this argument until their mother *interjected* that the size of the ears didn't matter, and they should take the dog for a walk.

UNIT SIX

SERV
Latin SERVARE, SERVATUM, "to save, keep"

PRESERVATION　(pre zer vā´ shən)　*n.*　The act or process of saving
L. pre, "beforehand," + servatum = *to save beforehand, to guard*
The *preservation* of wild areas in the United States is a very important idea.
syn: protection　　　　　　*ant:* disposal

CONSERVATIVE　(kən ser´ və tiv)　*adj.*　Not taking chances; disliking change; not extreme
L. con, "together," + servatum = *keeping together*
Betty tended to be *conservative* and cautious, while her brother Steven was more impulsive and adventurous.
syn: cautious　　　　　　*ant:* reckless

OBSERVANT　(ob zer´ vənt)　*adj.*　Paying careful attention to; noticing much
L. ob, "over," + servare = *to keep over, watch*
If you are *observant* enough, you may catch a glimpse of the rare hawk in your backyard.
syn: watchful　　　　　　*ant:* oblivious

STRICT
Latin STRINGERE, STRICTUM, "to bind"

CONSTRICT　(kən strikt´)　*v.*　To squeeze tightly
L. con, "together," + strictum = *to bind together*
The tight bandage *constricted* the patient's arm, reducing blood flow to the fingers.
syn: bind　　　　　　*ant:* loosen

RESTRICTION　(rē strik´ shən)　*n.*　Something that limits
L. re, "back," + strictum = *bound back*
If Norm doesn't put some *restrictions* on buying video games, he'll have no money left for gas to get to his favorite music store.
syn: check, curb　　　　　　*ant:* allowance

A person who is conservative is one who supports conditions as they are, resists social change, and sticks closely to tradition.

SOLUT
Latin SOLVERE, SOLUTUM, "to loosen, solve"

SOLUTION   (sə lōō´ shən)   *n.*   Something that answers or helps
The *solution* to traffic jams, it seems to me, is to install computerized stoplights.
syn: explanation   *ant*: complication

ABSOLUTE   (ab sə lōōt´)   *n.* Something that is certain; something that does
      not change
L. ab, "from," + solutum = *loosened from (all limit), complete, unchanging*
The only *absolute* in nature is that all living things will eventually die.
syn: constant   *ant*: variable

LIB, LIV
Latin LIBER, "free"

DELIVERANCE   (də liv´ ə rəns)   *n.*   Something that saves or helps
L. de, "away from," + liber = *freedom from*
The medicine appeared to give Melissa some *deliverance* from the pain.
syn: salvation

LIBERATE   (lib´ ər āt)   *v.*   To set free
The new governor refused to *liberate* any political prisoners.
syn: emancipate   *ant*: imprison

LIBERAL   (lib´ ər əl)   *adj.*   1. Giving in amount; plentiful
                                      2. Generous
1. Nigel asked for a *liberal* helping of mashed potatoes.
2. Malcolm was *liberal* in his praise for the new restaurant.
syn: unselfish   *ant*: ungiving

I like to DRIBBLE LIBERAL amounts of mustard on my hot dog.

▥ *To absolve (from ab, "from," + solvere = loosen from) is to release from guilt or blame. Some religious groups believe that people can take certain steps to be absolved from sin or wrongdoing. The process of forgiveness is called absolution.*

▥ *A liberal is a person who seeks change. The word is often used to mean the opposite of "conservative."*

EXERCISES - UNIT SIX

Exercise I. Complete the sentence in a way that shows you understand the meaning of the italicized vocabulary word.

1.   If you are *observant* during the tennis match, you will be able to see...

2.   John gave Louis a *liberal* helping of vegetables because...

3.   Many people feel that the *solution* to the problem of higher taxes is...

4.   Marcos believes in the *preservation* of historic buildings because...

5.   My sister is very *conservative* when it comes to spending money because...

6.   We hoped that the passing car would be our *deliverance*, but instead...

7.   The principal placed new *restrictions* on the students because...

8.   Because Barry's throat *constricts* when he eats peanuts or peanut butter, he...

9.   In order to *liberate* the citizens on the island, the soldiers...

10.   The teacher said that certain things, like the speed of light, are *absolutes* because...

Exercise II. Fill in the blank with the best word from the choices below. One word will not be used.

absolute   liberate   deliverance   constricted

1.   When Beth saw the rabbits in a cage at the pet store, she desperately wanted to _____ them.

2.   The rope _____ my hands so that blood stopped flowing to them.

3.   When I lost an important homework assignment, I looked to the snowstorm that was coming as _____.

Fill in the blank with the best word from the choices below. One word will not be used.

solution   preservation   liberal   observant

4.   Leonard has dedicated himself to the _____ of old filmstrips that might otherwise be thrown out.

5.   We worked on the math problem a long time before we found a(n) _____.

6.   As a private detective, George found that he had to be very _____ of his surroundings.

Fill in the blank with the best word from the choices below. One word will not be used.

liberal   absolutes   restriction   conservative   observant

7.   Jacob found himself under heavy _____ when he broke his parents' curfew.

8.   Without _____ donations, we will never be able to build the new playground.

9.   It is important to be _____ when it comes to using electricity so that we don't waste energy.

10.   There seem to be no _____ in the weather forecast; things are constantly changing.

Exercise III. Choose the set of words that best completes the sentence.

1.   Pete tried to _____ himself from the seatbelt that tightly _____ him.
      A. constrict; liberated
      B. liberate; constricted
      C. absolute; liberated
      D. restrict; delivered

2.   While Sarah is _____ with her Halloween candy and often gives it away, Rebecca takes a more _____ approach.
      A. liberal; conservative
      B. observant; conservative
      C. absolute; liberal
      D. observant; absolute

3.   Just when we started to think there was no _____ for the problem of the drought, a sudden rain-storm was our _____.
      A. solution; absolute
      B. deliverance; restriction
      C. restriction; preservation
      D. solution; deliverance

4.   The survival of the rain forests is not a(n) _____; it depends on our efforts at _____.
      A. absolute; deliverance
      B. solution; restriction
      C. deliverance; restriction
      D. absolute; preservation

5.   Because Bob was not a very _____ driver, he did not notice when new traffic _____ went into effect.
      A. observant; restrictions
      B. conservative; solutions
      C. liberal; preservations
      D. observant; absolutes

Exercise IV. Complete the sentence by inferring information about the italicized word from its context.

1.   If Julie is especially *observant* while she watches the football game, she may…

2.   One *restriction* on teenagers you might remove if you were the mayor of your city is…

3.   If your throat is *constricted,* you will probably feel…

Exercise V. Fill in the blank with the word from the Unit that best completes the sentence, using the root
we supply as a clue. Then, answer the questions that follow the paragraphs.

Imagine green walls and brown carpets. Imagine going to the bank to get a loan for college and being refused. Imagine being at the mercy of a landlord when bugs crawl across your floor. Any of these scenarios can occur when you rent a home. Owning a home is the way to avoid these situations. In addition, many other financial and personal benefits come with home ownership.

Several of these benefits are financial ones. Unless you pay cash for your home, you will borrow money from a financial institution, usually a bank, and then pay it back with interest. As you pay your mortgage payments, you owe the lender less and less and own more of your home. This ownership is called "equity." If you go to the bank to borrow money to buy a car or to pay your school tuition, your equity will help you qualify for the loan. The lender can see you are trustworthy and responsible in paying back your loans, and the lender could repossess your house if you do not make the loan payments. Therefore, equity gives you the opportunity to borrow more money.

Owning a home can also result in tax savings. At the end of every year, all citizens of our country must pay taxes. One type of tax is based on yearly income. When you own a home, you can subtract the interest you pay on the home from your income; consequently, you will have to pay less in taxes to the government.

Owning a home not only makes financial sense—it also has personal rewards, like a sense of stability and of community. Owning gives you the opportunity to plant "roots." You become a part of a group of people who unite for the _____ (SERV) of the neighborhood. You begin to feel a sense of belonging. People who rent homes do not have this stability. Neighbors are constantly moving in and out. People are robbed of their privacy, and they must rely on other people to take care of common household problems, like leaky faucets or pests. If you have a lax landlord, you are in for frustration.

Then, too, owning a home can bring you pride and independence. When you rent, you have to accept the dwelling as is. Even if the walls are green and the carpet is brown, you have to rent what you can afford, but buying a home _____ (LIB) you. You can purchase a home in your price range and then decorate it however you please. After years of yardwork and home repairs, you can know that everything you have is yours.

Owning a home can be your _____ (LIV) from the hassles of noisy neighboring tenants and unreliable landlords. You become a part of the community, and you are given equity in your home that you can use to improve your life in many other ways. It is obvious that buyers reap many benefits from the purchase of a home.

1.   Which of the following situations, can, according to the passage, be avoided by home ownership?
      A. low interest rates
      B. leaky faucets
      C. a sense of pride
      D. independence

2.   When might the author think it is appropriate to rent?
      A. when you want a sense of belonging
      B. when you are staying in an area only for a few months
      C. when you pay income taxes
      D. when you want independence from a landlord

3.   What does the passage conclude about home ownership?
      A. Home ownership leads to more taxes.
      B. Home ownership creates dependence on others.
      C. Home ownership is beneficial.
      D. Home ownership creates too much debt.

4.   Which benefit below is NOT a financial benefit?
      A. equity
      B. tax relief
      C. approved loans
      D. independence

Exercise VI. Drawing on your knowledge of roots and words in context, read the following selection and define the *italicized* words. If you cannot figure out the meaning of the words on your own, look them up in a dictionary. Note that *re* means "back."

Ted was a *reserved* student; he rarely spoke up in class, left the other students alone, and spent his recess time quietly reading a book. However, when the principal announced that she was putting new *strictures* in place to keep the students' behavior in check, Ted felt that he had to speak up. He argued that since most of the kids were responsible and well-behaved, there was no need to tightly limit them with harsh rules.

UNIT SEVEN

LITER 6/11
Latin LITTERA, "letter"

LITERAL (lit´ ər əl)   *adj.*   Exactly true, rather than figurative or metaphorical
Our teacher told us that the poem had much more to offer than just a *literal* message about a sunrise.
syn: actual

LITERATE (lit´ ər it)   *adj.*   1. Able to read
                                        2. Well-read
1. The library set up a tutoring program to help people who were not *literate*.
2. Susan has read over 2,000 books and is one of the most *literate* people I know.

OBLITERATE (ə blit´ ə rāt)   *v.*   To completely destroy
Celia's nasty note *obliterated* all the positive feelings that Marcel had for her.
syn: erase   *ant*: build up

LOG 6/12
Greek LOGOS, "word, speech, idea, reason"

ILLOGICAL (ə loj´ ə kəl)   *adj.*   Not done according to reason
G. in, "not," + logos = *not according to reason*
As the two debaters got worked up, their arguments became more *illogical*.
syn: irrational   *ant*: sensible

ANALOGY (ə nâl´ ə jē)   *n.*   Comparison
G. ana, "according to," + logos = *according to reason*
The professor tried to think of an *analogy* to explain the rotation of the sun.

APOLOGETIC (ə päl ə jet´ ik)   *adj.*   Sorry; showing regret
G. apo, "from," + logos = *speech from*
The weatherman seemed *apologetic* about predicting clear skies the night before a nine-inch snowfall.
syn: regretful   *ant*: proud

GRAM, GRAPH 6/13
Greek GRAMMA, "letter, writing"
GRAPHEIN, "to write"

DIAGRAM (dī´ ə gram)   *v.*   To draw a detailed picture of; to map out
G. dia, "across, out" + gramma = *write out*
Not even the best students were able to *diagram* the solution to the math problem.
syn: sketch

We use obliterated when we want to say something has been completely destroyed. But it originally meant "to erase letters," as you would from a chalkboard or a sheet of paper.

The Greek logos has many different meanings, "word," "thought" and "reason." We can see the last meaning best in the English word logic, which describes orderly movement from one idea to another.

Apology is a word based on the "word" meaning of logos. An apologia, to the Greeks, was a speech given to get off of a charge of wrongdoing. One of the most famous was supposed to have been given by the Greek philosopher Socrates; his pupil, Plato, published a version of this speech.

PROGRAM   (prō´ grâm)   *v.*   To train; to teach
G. pro, "forth," + gramma = *write forth*
We were able to *program* our home security system to notify the police within ten seconds of a break-in.

BIOGRAPHICAL   (bī ə grâf´ ə kəl)   *adj.*   Describing one's life
G. bios, "life," + graphein = *to write about the life of*
The director's fifth movie was a *biographical* account of a famous jazz trumpeter.

SCRIPT, SCRIB 6/14
Latin SCRIBERE, SCRIPTUM, "to write"

DESCRIPTIVE   (də skrip´ tiv)   *adj.*   Giving details about; illustrating; explaining
L. de, "down," + scriptum = *written down*
Because the advertisement was not very *descriptive,* many people were confused about the product.

SUBSCRIBE   (sub skrīb´)   *v.*   To believe in; to feel approval or agreement
L. sub, "under," + scribere = *to write under*
Anyone who still *subscribes* to the idea that the sun revolves around the Earth simply does not want to believe the scientific facts.
syn: support   *ant*: oppose

MANUSCRIPT   (man´ ū skript)   *n.*   A handwritten document
L. manus, "hand," + scriptum = *handwritten*
The poet decided to burn all of her original *manuscripts.*

MAN, YOU STRIPPED the MANUSCRIPT of
all the important stuff.

The word subscribe means "to write under" or "to sign." If you sign a document, you are saying that you personally stand by the truth of that document.

While a manuscript is often written out or copied by hand, the word can also mean "a first copy of something." If an author types out a first version of a novel, it could be called a manuscript even though it came from a computer.

EXERCISES - UNIT SEVEN

Exercise I. Complete the sentence in a way that shows you understand the meaning of the italicized vocabulary word.

1.   Walter was *apologetic* about crashing the car because…

2.   Joseph does not *subscribe* to the President's ideas because…

3.   Because the asteroid may *obliterate* our entire town, we are feeling…

4.   It is important to remember that the *literal* meaning of a word can be different from…

5.   Tamara has written a *biographical* novel about the composer that will help readers understand…

6.   Researchers are studying the ancient *manuscript* in order to learn…

7.   Paul prepared a *diagram* of the car's engine for his students so they could…

8.   The robot's creator has *programmed* it to…

9.   In an effort to make the citizens of the country more *literate*, the government…

10.   I believe that buying a new car would be *illogical* because my old car…

11.   The professor used an *analogy* when discussing the Civil War to help his students…

12.   While on vacation in Alaska, Samantha wrote a *descriptive* letter to her sister so that…

Exercise II. Fill in the blank with the best word from the choices below. One word will not be used.

literal	subscribed	programmed	apologetic	obliterated

1.   Although Kim said that she was sorry for the mess, she did not seem very _____.

2.   Steve _____ to a religion that would not allow him to celebrate certain holidays.

3.   Because my car was _____ in the accident, I had to get a new one.

4.   The on-board computer could be _____ to do several things at once.

Fill in the blank with the best word from the choices below. One word will not be used.

diagram   literate   literal   manuscript   analogy

5.   Verne hoped to become more _____ by reading lots of books.

6.   The _____ of my novel has been sent to a publishing house for consideration.

7.   We gained a better understanding of the way the tiger moved by looking at a(n) _____ of its skeleton.

8.   The song's _____ meaning is very different from its poetic one.

Fill in the blank with the best word from the choices below. One word will not be used.

illogical   analogy   diagram   descriptive   biographical

9.   Although some people mistakenly think the movie is _____, it is not based on any person's life.

10. Some of the choices Cam has made seem totally _____, but they actually make sense when you ask about them.

11. Try as he might, Tim could not come up with a(n) _____ to describe the situation he had been in.

12. The policeman, looking for details that would lead to an arrest, asked the witness for a more _____ account of the crime.

Exercise III. Choose the set of words that best completes the sentence.

1.   If Serge's speech about the mechanical parrot is not _____ enough, he can draw you a(n) _____.
    A. biographical; manuscript
    B. literal; analogy
    C. descriptive; diagram
    D. illogical; program

2.   Even if you try to _____ your son Vincent to believe what you believe, he may not _____ to all of your ideas.
    A. subscribe; obliterate
    B. obliterate; program
    C. program; subscribe
    D. obliterate; subscribe

3.   Because few people in the ancient country were _____, the _____ had been read by only a handful of citizens.
   A.   diagram; analogy
   B.   literate; manuscript
   C.   illogical; diagram
   D.   biographical; manuscript

4.   Because the _____ meaning of the passage is hard to understand, our teacher used a(n) _____ to explain it.
   A.   descriptive; manuscript
   B.   illogical; manuscript
   C.   literal; analogy
   D.   apologetic; analogy

5.   Although Barney admitted that his actions had been strange and _____, he was not _____ about the situation.
   A.   illogical; apologetic
   B.   descriptive; biographical
   C.   apologetic; literate
   D.   descriptive; biographical

Exercise IV. Complete the sentence by inferring information about the italicized word from its context.

1.   When the news claims the town was *obliterated* in only a few seconds, you might suspect…

2.   If three-year-old Sharon believes everything in too *literal* a way, you probably shouldn't…

3.   One *analogy* that might help explain photosynthesis is…

Exercise V. Fill in the blank with the word from the Unit that best completes the sentence, using the root we supply as a clue. Then, answer the questions that follow the paragraphs.

Global warming. Dwindling water supplies. Overpopulation. Starvation. These are just a few of the problems facing our planet and its residents. Even if people change the way they use and share resources, and even if the growth of the population is slowed, there will continue to be conflicts between how people would like to use the Earth and what the planet has to offer.

A highly creative solution to this problem would be to find ways to let humans live in other places throughout the solar system. The moon may be a poor choice, since changing its mass through civilization will affect its gravitational relationship with Earth, but Mars is definitely a possibility. Colonization of Mars would have three primary benefits for the Earth: reduced demands on this planet's resources, increased interest in alternative forms of energy and agriculture, and a continued existence for the human species in the event of a catastrophe on Earth.

If there is water on Mars, it would not be _____ (LOG) to colonize Mars fairly soon. Right now, it takes six to nine months to reach the planet from Earth—not much more time than it took to go from Europe to North America in the 16th-century era of exploration. Every person who could exist on Mars, independent of the resources of Earth, would give our planet a chance to renew itself.

Another reason to colonize Mars would be to speed up the discovery of new sources of energy. As long as the world economy depends on oil as an energy source, there will be problems like pollution and shrinking resources. Moving to a planet without oil would immediately make new sources of energy necessary. If these sources work well on Mars, they would be easy to use on Earth as well.

An asteroid or comet that strikes the Earth could _____ (LITER) our planet's population of 6.5

billion. While the odds are astronomical that an object from outer space could harm Earth, over time, such a collision is unavoidable; in fact, many scientists think that this is what killed all of the dinosaurs. In addition, humans possess weapons that could destroy the planet itself; in the event of a nuclear war, the Earth would be destroyed or made impossible to live on. Establishing a colony on Mars would ensure that the human species could exist even after the destruction of its planet.

Clearly, colonization of another planet would bring many advantages to humanity. The earth could only benefit from having fewer people to support, and having alternate energy sources would certainly not be a bad thing. Also, colonization would give the human race a place of escape if the Earth were in danger. The costs would be high, but the benefits could be priceless.

1. Which of the following would be the BEST title for this essay?
   A. "The Importance of New Energy Sources"
   B. "Mission to Mars: The Search for Water"
   C. "Recreating the New World in Space"
   D. "Three Reasons to Stay on Earth"

2. According to the passage, colonization of Mars would
   A. be disastrous for Earth.
   B. be beneficial for Mars.
   C. make the chance of an asteroid strike more likely.
   D. reduce demands on Earth.

3. Which of the following BEST summarizes the author's main idea?
   A. Oil companies would lose money if alternate sources of energy were discovered.
   B. Human colonization of Mars would allow the human species to survive longer.
   C. Human colonization of Mars would allow the resources of the earth to last forever.
   D. The costs of colonizing Mars would be unbelievably high.

4. Which sentence best states the point of this essay?
   A. the last sentence of the third paragraph
   B. the last sentence of the second paragraph
   C. the first sentence of the last paragraph
   D. the last sentence of the first paragraph

Exercise VI. Drawing on your knowledge of roots and words in context, read the following selection and define the *italicized* words. If you cannot figure out the meaning of the words on your own, look them up in a dictionary. Note that *post* means "after," and *al*, from *ad*, means "to."

In a *postscript* to her poem about people dancing and listening to music, the author explains why she feels it is so important for words in every line to begin with the same sound. She says that this *alliteration* helps the reader hear and feel the same things as the people in the poem. Once you have read the poem, read her explanation and see if you agree with it.

UNIT EIGHT

CESS
Latin CEDERE, CESSUM, "to go, to yield"

ACCESSIBLE   (ak ses´ ə bəl)   *adj.*   Able to be reached or understood
L. ad, "to," + cessum = *come to*
My school was not *accessible* because a huge tree was blocking the road.

SUCCESSION   (suk sesh´ ən)   *n.*   A group of things that follow one another
L. sub, "up from under," + cessum = *to go up from under, climb up to, follow*
A *succession* of bad leaders had made the country unstable.
syn: series

PROCESSION   (prə sesh´ ən)   *n.*   A group that moves together
L. pro, "forth," + cessum = *going forth*
The beautiful *procession* of animals and performers from the circus persuaded us to buy tickets as soon as possible.

GRAD, GRESS
Latin GRADI, GRESSUS, "to go, progress"

TRANSGRESS   (tranz gres´ ən)   *v.*   To go against a law or rule
L. trans, "across," + gressus = *going across (boundaries or rules)*
For every rule that the children *transgress*, their mother fines them a nickel.
syn: violate   *ant:* obey

PROGRESSION   (prə gresh´ ən)   *n.*   A going forth, a movement toward
L. pro, "forth," + gressus = *going forth*
Because Arlene practiced extremely hard, her *progression* from amateur to professional dancer took her only one year.

GRADUAL   (gra´ jōō əl)   *adj.*   Happening over a period of time
Everyone was happy to see the *gradual* but steady increase in the number of students going to college.
syn: eventual   *ant:* immediate

▥ *The Latin* cedere *means both to "go forth," as you do when you walk from one place to another, and "to give way, to yield." This is why we get the word* proceed, *which means "go forward," and* cease, *which means "stop," from the same root.*

▥ *You have probably heard the word* succeed *used to mean "do well" or "win." It also "to come after," especially, "to follow someone else into a position of authority." Thus, a prince might* succeed *his father on the throne; one president* succeeds *the next.*

IT
Latin IRE, ITUM, "to go"

AMBITION   (âm bish´ ən)   *n.*   A desire to succeed or be powerful
L. ambi, "around," + itum = *a going around*
Larry's *ambition* is to be an Elvis Presley impersonator, which is surprising because he cannot sing.

TRANSIT   (tranz´ it)   *n.*   The act or process of moving from one place to another
L. trans, "across," + itum = *a going across*
The package is now in *transit*, heading for New Jersey.

CUR, COURS
Latin CURRERE, CURSUM, "to run"

OCCURRENCE   (ə kûr´ əns)   *n.*   An instance
L. ob, "towards," + currere = *running towards*
Fred wasn't sure, but he felt JoAnn was referring to the *occurrence* that took place yesterday.

COURSE   (kôrs)   *v.*   To flow; to stream
Once the pipe is fixed, water will *course* through at about a gallon a minute.
syn: gush

CURRENCY   (kûr´ ən sē)   *n.*   Money, especially paper money
Confederate money that was used in the Civil War has no real value today, except to *currency* collectors.

RECURRENT   (rē kûr´ ənt)   *adj.*   Happening many times
L. re, "again," + currere = *to run again*
In Paul's *recurrent* nightmare, which wakes him up frequently, cannibals are chasing him through the jungle.
syn: repeated   *ant*: one-time

Shocking himself became a RECURRENT event.

> ⫸ *In ancient Rome, candidates for political office walked ("itum") around ("ambi") to ask for votes. In modern day,* ambition *does not have to be political; you, for instance, could have great* ambitions *for your science fair project or your career.*

EXERCISES - UNIT EIGHT

Exercise I. Complete the sentence in a way that shows you understand the meaning of the italicized vocabulary word.

1.   In order to make the difficult book more *accessible* to readers, the author...

2.   Water could not *course* through the hose because...

3.   The *procession* of funeral-goers started at the funeral home because...

4.   Jay's *ambition* is to be student body president because...

5.   The country's *currency* had lost some of its value because...

6.   Darlene does not wish to *transgress* the...

7.   The disappearance of the rain forest has not been *gradual*, but...

8.   Doctors followed the *progression* of the patient's disease by...

9.   When Mike learned that there had been an *occurrence* of water poisoning in his town, he...

10.   While the package was in *transit*, some of its contents...

11.   Justin had *recurrent* headaches that...

12.   Our class had a *succession* of substitute teachers because...

Exercise II. Fill in the blank with the best word from the choices below. One word will not be used.

course   progress   accessible   gradual   currency

1.   Because of the Internet, information that was once unavailable is now _____ to everyone.

2.   The _____ increase in rainfall led the city's sewers to slowly fill up with water.

3.   When we crossed the border into Spain, we had to exchange all of our French _____.

4.   The doctors were happy to see blood _____ through the patient's veins after the arm had been sewn back on.

Fill in the blank with the best word from the choices below. One word will not be used.

occurrence   transit   succession   progression   ambition

5.   A new _____ system is needed to carry people from one end of the city to the other.

6.   As the reporter said, the snowstorm was a strange _____ in the hot desert town.

7.   It was difficult to follow the _____ of notes in the musical piece because they skipped all over the place.

8.   The _____ of kings ended when King Frank was killed in battle.

Fill in the blank with the best word from the choices below. One word will not be used.

recurrent   ambitions   successions   procession   transgressed

9.   Geraldine was given a new punishment for every rule she _____.

10.   For someone with as many _____ as Pauline, a simple desk job will never be good enough.

11.   Death, good and evil, and love are _____ ideas in the novel.

12.   We saw a(n) _____ of automobiles following the President in the parade.

Exercise III. Choose the set of words that best completes the sentence.

1.   The idea that health care should be _____ to everyone was _____ in the President's speech.
    A.   gradual; recurrent
    B.   accessible; recurrent
    C.   recurrent; gradual
    D.   accessible; gradual

2.   A(n) _____ of disasters led to a(n) _____ decline in the town's population.
    A.   occurrence; accessible
    B.   procession; accessible
    C.   ambition; recurrent
    D.   succession; gradual

3.   The _____ of cars was in _____ from the park to the beach.
    A.   procession; transit
    B.   progression; ambition
    C.   occurrence; succession
    D.   currency; transit

4. You may have a lot of _____ and desire to succeed, but it doesn't mean you can _____ all the rules of our company.
    A. succession; transgress
    B. currency; course
    C. ambition; transgress
    D. ambition; course

5. The _____ of the blood as it _____ through the patient's veins was represented by a series of arrows.
    A. transit; transgressed
    B. progression; coursed
    C. currency; coursed
    D. currency; transgressed

Exercise IV. Complete the sentence by inferring information about the italicized word from its context.

1. If Morgan notices a *gradual* increase in the temperature outside, he could believe that…

2. If the President declares that all Federal buildings should be *accessible* to wheelchairs,…

3. If the criminal makes a *progression* from burglary to assault, police might infer that…

Exercise V. Fill in the blank with the word from the Unit that best completes the sentence, using the root we supply as a clue. Then, answer the questions that follow the paragraphs.

As you grow in maturity and social skills, you naturally want to branch out and do interesting things with your friends. One of the finest things young people can do today is volunteer in their communities. Volunteering gives you an opportunity to interact with adults who provide necessary services in your community. Maybe there are refugees who need legal or medical services that are not _____(CESS) to them, but have nobody willing to take the time to show them the way to the offices. You could be that person, and you could learn during the course of your service how people of other cultures live by talking with these people in need. You might even make some lifelong friends!

Maybe you are naturally talented as a game player or computer genius. What if you took those skills into a local nursing home and taught senior citizens how to use e-mail or type on a computer? Soon, they would be able to increase their contact with the outside world. You could help them escape from the boredom of everyday life in a nursing home. That would certainly make both you and those you help feel pretty special.

We all know we are lucky to live the way we do. It isn't without cost, though. Citizens have to contribute in a meaningful way to their society, or the society will not prosper. Just as you should contribute to the welfare of your home and your school, you should contribute to the general welfare of your community. Join a club or service organization, help adults pick up trash along the interstate, help deliver meals to the housebound, visit the sick, volunteer at a hospital, read to a blind person, help rescue abandoned pets, clean up a riverbed, etc. The list is endless, and the rewards are great. They may not be financial, but the pride, character and self-esteem you will gain will more than make up for the lack of funds. Your community will be a better place, your contribution will not go unnoticed, and your friends will want to join you as you make a significant contribution to the well-being of your fellow human. Who knows–your volunteering may blossom into a field of study, leading you on a _____ (GRAD) path to becoming a certified professional caregiver. Volunteer! You'll be glad you did.

1. Why does the author of this passage encourage volunteerism?
    A. It is the duty of all adults.
    B. It gives someone a chance to give back to the community.
    C. It is a way to build character.
    D. Both B and C

2. According to the article, a young person could volunteer to do all of the following EXCEPT
    A. wait on tables.
    B. rescue stray animals.
    C. teach how to use e-mail.
    D. pick up trash.

3. What could be considered a "reward" of volunteering?
    A. Increased self-esteem
    B. Improvement of the community
    C. Cultural awareness
    D. All the above

4. The author of this article is more likely to be from _____ than a large city.
    A. America
    B. a small town
    C. Neither A nor B
    D. It is impossible to tell from the passage.

5. The passage could be best categorized as
    A. descriptive.
    B. scientific.
    C. persuasive.
    D. dramatic.

Exercise VI. Drawing on your knowledge of roots and words in context, read the following selection and define the *italicized* words. If you cannot figure out the meaning of the words on your own, look them up in a dictionary. Note that *ex* means "out" or "beyond."

The money the Lee family spent on vacation this year *exceeded* their summer budget. They went to Paris and had such a wonderful time that they completely forgot about their wallets. When they got home and saw that they had spent too much, they decided next year's trip will have to be cheaper. They will probably take a brief *excursion* to Yellowstone National Park, which is not far from their home.

UNIT NINE

FORT
Latin FORTIS, "strong"

EFFORTLESS   (ef´ ərt ləs)   *adj.*   Not requiring much work
One of the gymnasts struggled through his performance, while the other completed his routine with *effortless* grace.
syn: easy   *ant:* difficult

FORTIFY   (fôr´ tə fī)   *v.*   To make stronger
Most cereal makers *fortify* their products with extra vitamins.
syn: build up   *ant:* weaken

FORTITUDE   (fôr´ ti tōōd)   *n.*   Strength of mind or character
Spending a month in the wilderness camp requires a *fortitude* that many people do not possess.
syn: courage   *ant:* cowardice

TEG
Latin INTEGER, "whole, unbroken"

INTEGRATE   (in´ tə grāt)   *v.*   1. To bring together
                                      2. To work something into
1. The new comic's routine *integrates* material from several of his previous shows.
2. Ingrid tries hard to *integrate* her doctor's recommendations into her daily activities.
syn: blend   *ant:* separate

INTEGRITY   (in teg´ rə tē)   *n.*   Honesty; moral soundness
Bobby's *integrity* is such that he once returned a briefcase worth hundreds of dollars to the owner instead of keeping it.
syn: goodness

DISINTEGRATE   (dis in´ tə grāt)   *v.*   To fall apart
L. dis, "not," + integer = *not whole*
Lisa's relationship with Jeremy began to *disintegrate* as soon as she saw his terrible table manners.
syn: crumble   *ant:* hold up

FIRM
Latin FIRMARE, FIRMATUM, "to strengthen, give strength"
FIRMUS, "firm"

AFFIRMATIVE (ə firm´ ə tiv) *adj.* Agreeing with; supporting
L. ad, "to," + firmatum = *give strength to*
An *affirmative* vote helped the bill become a law.
syn: confirming   *ant*: denying

CONFIRM (kən firm´) *v.* To settle as true
L. con, "completely," + firmare = *to completely strengthen*
The names of people who died in the earthquake could not be *confirmed* until those who were injured were identified.
syn: verify

INFIRM (in firm´) *adj.* Not in good health; not well
L. in, "not," + firmus = *not strong*
Roberto thought his grandfather looked too *infirm* to do much, but the elderly man certainly could throw a ball accurately.
syn: frail   *ant*: strong

VAL, VALID
Latin VALERE, VALITURUS, "to be strong; be worth"
VALIDUS, "strong"

INVALUABLE (in val´ yə bəl) *adj.* Very helpful or useful
L. in, "not," + valere = *beyond value*
Clark's advice about using the computer was *invaluable* to us.
syn: priceless   *ant*: worthless

EVALUATE (ē val´ ū āt) *v.* To judge; to size up
The judges barely had time to *evaluate* one performer before the next one began singing.
syn: analyze

INVALID (in val´ əd) *adj.* Not good enough; not correct
L. in, "not," + validus = *not strong*
If that answer is *invalid*, what is the right one?

VALIDATE (val´ i dāt) *v.* To declare good; to accept as good /accept as proven correct
The teacher tries to *validate* her students' ideas because she wants them to be confident.
syn: approve   *ant*: refuse

Christmas is a VALID DATE to travel, so we'll VALIDATE your ticket.

Ⅲ *In addition to these words, we get the English* value *from the Latin "valere." Value is a measure of how strong or good something is; the value of a book can be measured by the good it does you, for instance, and the value of a shelter by how much it protects you from the rain. To evaluate is to judge the strength or goodness of something, while invaluable means "so good that its worth cannot be evaluated."*

EXERCISES - UNIT NINE

Exercise I. Complete the sentence in a way that shows you understand the meaning of the italicized vocabulary word.

1.   The soldiers decided to *fortify* the outside wall of the castle with…

2.   We were unable to *validate* the witness' account of the robbery because…

3.   When her theory was proven *invalid*, Melissa said that…

4.   The house may *disintegrate* under the heavy rain if it…

5.   The skater's *effortless* performance made audience members…

6.   The elephants in the zoo were *infirm* as a result of…

7.   Noah was known as a man of great *integrity* in the office because…

8.   The company's newsletter proved to be *invaluable* when…

9.   When Jackie made an *affirmative* statement about the size of the fish, Frank…

10.   The weatherman *confirmed* our fears about rain on the day of the picnic, so we…

11.   The software company will try to *integrate* its old product with…

12.   The *fortitude* with which Jake faced his surgery showed us that…

13.   The committee will *evaluate* the Mayor's plan and tell us…

Exercise II. Fill in the blank with the best word from the choices below. One word will not be used.

disintegrate   invaluable   confirm   fortify   invalid

1.   The park ranger gave us some _____ information that saved us lots of time on the hike.

2.   The mayor will not _____ the rumor that he is planning to retire in February.

3.   Because they had been cooked too long, the vegetables began to _____, and soon they were nothing but mush.

4.   Sir John was a powerful knight, but he wisely chose to _____ himself with extra armor.

Fill in the blank with the best word from the choices below. One word will not be used.

integrating affirmative confirm effortless invalid

5. Though the flight of birds seems graceful and _____, it actually requires a lot of energy and work.

6. The choir worked on _____ its singing with the playing of the orchestra.

7. When asked, the witness gave a(n) _____ comment about the time of the robberies.

8. The coupon was _____ because it had expired several months before.

Fill in the blank with the best word from the choices below. One word will not be used.

validate infirm integrity evaluate fortify fortitude

9. The scouts promised to use _____ and honesty in everything they did.

10. The members of the writing group tried to _____ each other by using positive feedback.

11. Fred was an old and _____ cat, but once in a while he would run and play.

12. One positive effect of having inner _____ is that you rely on yourself.

13. Dennis wanted some more time to _____ the results.

Exercise III. Choose the set of words that best completes the sentence.

1. Because of his _____ and loyalty, Will is a(n) _____ employee of the company.
   A. fortitude; effortless
   B. invalid; infirm
   C. fortitude; affirmative
   D. integrity; invaluable

2. My uncle is elderly and _____, so his concern about slipping and falling is hardly _____.
   A. invalid; infirm
   B. infirm; invalid
   C. fortitude; invalid
   D. invalid; fortitude

3. The spokesman would not _____ rumors about his client going to jail, but he did _____ that police were investigating.
   A. validate; disintegrate
   B. validate; confirm
   C. integrate; validate
   D. evaluate; disintegrate

4. We were amazed at the _____ way Jake managed to _____ new activities into his already busy schedule.
    A. effortless; integrate
    B. invaluable; disintegrate
    C. effortless; confirm
    D. invaluable; fortify

5. Unless you _____ your sand castle with twigs and stones, it will completely _____ as soon as the next wave comes along.
    A. evaluate; integrate
    B. validate; confirm
    C. confirm; fortify
    D. fortify; disintegrate

Exercise IV. Complete the sentence by inferring information about the italicized word from its context.

1. If Paulie feels his baseball card collection is *invaluable*, he might...

2. The government wants airplane makers to *fortify* their planes against hijackers by...

3. Because Theo won the race *effortlessly*, the fans might guess that...

Exercise V. Fill in the blank with the word from the Unit that best completes the sentence, using the root we supply as a clue. Then, answer the questions that follow the paragraphs.

Are you looking for a new sport that is cooler than karate, skateboarding, or soccer? Perhaps you are thinking about what you might want to be when you get older, and playing sports has entered your mind. Well, you are in luck. Start thinking about scuba diving and _____ (VAL) the possibilities of the sport for present and future.

Scuba diving is a sport that can be enjoyed by men, women and children. Individuals between the ages of 10 and 15 can earn Junior Open Water Diver certification; people 15 and older can earn Open Water Diver certification. Kids younger than 10 can become Bubblemakers or Scuba Rangers. Almost anyone in good health can participate as long as they meet the age requirements.

To start scuba diving, you will need a mask, a snorkel, a pair of diving fins, your swimsuit, towel, and notebook. A great amount of time will be spent in the pool working on your skills. You will want to take notes on safety considerations, equipment checks, etc. so that you can _____ (TEG) the information from your teacher's class with sessions in the pool. For example, the number one cause of scuba equipment damage and _____ (TEG) is failure to soak the equipment in fresh water after a

dive trip. You and a dive buddy will be taught how to familiarize yourselves with the dive site before each dive and how to summon help if you have a problem. You will develop a backup strategy in case things do not work out as intended. There will be a lot of things to write in your notebook!

Accomplished scuba divers do more than just check out the fish! Scuba divers explore and learn new things about the oceans, lakes and rivers of the world. They dive for fun to see sharks and dolphins. They can explore coral reefs, build underwater structures, and salvage ships. Scuba divers can specialize in night diving, underwater photography, and/or wreck diving.

If scuba becomes a favorite activity, you may want to invest additional time and effort to become a commercial diver, a scientific diver, or a military diver. Those who dive for a living get paid well for diving in the waters of the world, and have the freedom to travel to many different countries. Most professional divers report that the most _____ (VAL) reward of choosing the career is the personal satisfaction and pride that come from knowing that they have done a job extremely well.

1. The best title for this selection would be
   A. "Scuba Diving for Fun and Profit."
   B. "Scuba Diving Lessons."
   C. "How to Become a Scuba Diver."
   D. "Scuba Diving's Hidden Dangers."

2. The author of this passage would probably support which of the following statements?
   A. As a sport, scuba diving is reserved for those who are extremely athletic and well-coordinated.
   B. The expenses associated with scuba diving far outweigh the advantages of participating in the sport.
   C. A career in scuba diving can satisfy any adventure seeker's desires.
   D. Professional scuba divers earn incomes that barely meet their expenses.

3. Based on the information you read in the passage, which of the following statements is NOT true?
   A. Scuba diving is safe up to a depth of six hundred feet.
   B. Scuba divers carry out research on marine life.
   C. Scuba divers always become specialists in search and recovery.
   D. Scuba diving is something that people of all ages can grow to like.

4. The author suggests rinsing diving equipment with fresh water after each dive. What is the main reason this suggestion is made?
   A. Underwater photography requires clean gear.
   B. All diving schools say to do it.
   C. Fresh water lubricates the flexible seals on diving equipment.
   D. Equipment not washed in this way will fall apart sooner.

Exercise VI. Drawing on your knowledge of roots and words in context, read the following selection and define the *italicized* words. If you cannot figure out the meaning of the words on your own, look them up in a dictionary. Note that *pre* means "before, over."

The members of the swim team believe they will *prevail* in the championship meet because they have a great captain in Jim Smith. He is both strong and fast in individual and relay events, but his real *forte* is in organizing and cheering on the team. Without his strength as a leader, the team would fall apart. But with Jim, they are the favorites for the district trophy.

VOCABULARY FROM LATIN AND GREEK ROOTS

UNIT TEN

PUT
Latin PUTARE, PUTATUM, "to think, determine"

REPUTATION   (rep ū tā´ shən)   *n.* An idea held by the public about something
   or someone
L. re, "again," + putare = *to think again, to think over*
Many dogs have *reputations* for biting, but the fault is usually in the animal's
upbringing and training.

COMPUTE   (kəm pūt´)   *v.* To figure out an amount or number
L. com, "with," + putatum = *to determine with (calculation)*
Before there were calculators, people had to *compute* most math problems on
paper.
syn: calculate

FID
Latin FIDERE, FISUS, "to believe, trust"

CONFIDENT   (kon´ fə dənt)   *adj.* Sure; certain
The officer said she was *confident* that the robbery would be solved, and a short
time later, it was.
syn: secure   *ant*: unsure

CONFIDANTE   (kon fə dänt´)   *n.* Someone to whom one tells a secret
Even when Alicia was a teenager, she used her stuffed teddy bear as her *confidante* and told it every secret she had.

SENT, SENS
Latin SENTIRE, SENSUM, "to feel"

SENTIMENTAL (sen tə men´ təl) *adj.*   Showing or causing a lot of emotion
The dress was probably worthless, but to Eli's grandmother, it had great *sentimental* value.
syn: romantic   *ant:* factual

SENSIBLE (sen´ sə bəl) *adj.*   Smart and practical
When the snow forced them to turn the car around, Mr. Kellmer reminded his wife that going up the mountain in the first place was not very *sensible*.

SENSATION (sen sā´ shən) *n.*   A feeling or experience
As the drug began to take effect, I felt a tingling *sensation* creep upwards from my feet.

CRED, CREED
Latin CREDERE, CREDITUM, "to believe"

INCREDIBLE (in kred´ ə bəl) *adj.*   Unbelievable
L. in, "not," + credere = *not able to be believed*
It seemed *incredible* to the teacher that everyone in class got the exact same answer to test question three, so she suspected cheating.

DISCREDIT (dis kre´ dit) *v.* To take away belief or trust in
L. dis, "not," + creditum = *not believe*
The car company tried to *discredit* its competitors by claiming their cars were unsafe to drive.
syn: reject   *ant:* support

CREED (krēd) *n.* A statement of belief
"Treat others as you would like to be treated" is one of the easiest *creeds* to live by.

Ⅲ *You may also see* sensible *used to mean "aware" or "feeling." The sentence "I was sensible of a very bad pain in my head" means that I felt the pain; "I was sensible and did not spend all my money," though, means that I did the smart thing and saved my cash.*

The guy who didn't believe anything was in NEED of a CREED.

EXERCISES - UNIT TEN

Exercise I. Complete the sentence in a way that shows you understand the meaning of the italicized vocabulary word.

1.   Bill got a *reputation* for being an honest man when he...

2.   The reporter who broke the story about the chickens was *discredited* by...

3.   Arthur felt *confident* that he could win the track meet because...

4.   I often had the *sensation* that I was flying or gliding when I...

5.   Reginald said that the storm had been *incredible* because...

6.   Olivia is my *confidante*, so I often tell her...

7.   All the men on the ship lived and died by the same *creed* because...

8.   Angie was always *sentimental* when it came to weddings because...

9.   Because Janet was not very *sensible* when it came to money...

10. In order to *compute* the budget for this year, the accountant...

Exercise II. Fill in the blank with the best word from the choices below. One word will not be used.

compute   incredible   sensible   reputation

1.   Deirdre had a good _____ among her teachers because she was always cheerful and ready to learn.

2.   We tried to _____ the number of seats needed at the wedding reception by listing all the people who had agreed to come.

3.   When Francine saw the _____ meal Ken had prepared, she could hardly believe her eyes.

Fill in the blank with the best word from the choices below. One word will not be used.

confident   confidante   sensation   sensible

4.   When my _____ at work left for another job, I had no one with whom I could share my thoughts.

5.   My father told me to be _____ when buying a new car and not buy one just for looks.

6.   Izzy was surprised by the _____ of numbness in her legs when she awoke that morning.

Fill in the blank with the best word from the choices below. One word will not be used.

sentimental   creed   confident   discredited   computed

7.   Although Troy was not very _____ in his own skateboarding abilities at first, he grew braver as he got more practice.

8.   Whenever my family watches old home movies, we all get _____ and teary-eyed.

9.   Before he could take office as chairman of the club, Henry was asked to recite its _____.

10.   Although many people once believed that the Earth was flat, science eventually _____ the idea.

Exercise III. Choose the set of words that best completes the sentence.

1.   Because the scientist has a(n) _____ for not telling the truth, we should probably _____ her latest announcement.
      A.   reputation; discredit
      B.   sensation; compute
      C.   confidante; discredit
      D.   reputation; compute

2.   While I am glad you are _____ in your knowledge of the city streets, it seems only _____ to take along a map when you travel.
      A.   incredible; sensible
      B.   sentimental; sensible
      C.   incredible; sentimental
      D.   confident; sensible

3.   When I told my _____ at the office that someone had taken some money, she _____ the total amount that had been stolen.
      A.   creed; discredited
      B.   confidante; computed
      C.   reputation; discredited
      D.   sensation; computed

4. It may sound _____ or untrue, but Stella often has the _____ of flying when she's just walking along.
    A. incredible; sensation
    B. sentimental; confidante
    C. confident; reputation
    D. sensible; reputation

5. When reciting the Scouts' _____, which he had first pledged as a boy, my father became _____ and spoke fondly about his memories of scouting.
    A. creed; confident
    B. confidante; confident
    C. reputation; incredible
    D. creed; sentimental

Exercise IV. Complete the sentence by inferring information about the italicized word from its context.

1. If Gabriel feels that Laura is his *confidante*, he could easily…

2. The theater owner felt that the movie must have been too *sentimental* because…

3. Since Angel thinks his *reputation* is the most valuable thing he has, he might…

Exercise V. Fill in the blank with the word from the Unit that best completes the sentence, using the root we supply as a clue. Then, answer the questions that follow the paragraphs.

The death penalty has long been a favored punishment for those who commit murder. In fact, advocates often feel _____ (FID) in taking the life of someone who took someone else's life. Others call upon the death penalty to act as a deterrent to violent crimes. However, most arguments in favor of the death penalty can easily be _____ (CRED). In fact, criminologists and police officers do not credit the death penalty with reducing violent crime. In states with the death penalty, the murder rate is no lower than in states without it. It may be that when the state itself commits a killing, even in the name of justice, the death loses the sense of horror that should rightfully accompany it.

Moreover, it is not the case that justice is being served by the death penalty, for it is not true that the worst criminals receive it. It is true, though, that the death penalty is primarily administered to a particular type of person. Prosecutors are more likely to seek the death penalty if the offender is black and the victim is white. Additionally, most people who are put to death are poor. They cannot afford their own attorneys, so they must rely on public defenders, some of whom may be incompetent or lazy. Furthermore, the death penalty is applied differently in different jurisdictions, that is, from place to place. Overall, the use of the death penalty is inconsistent and unfair.

Of course, citizens demand justice in punishing criminals. However, justice, for death penalty advocates, means revenge in equal measure: a life for a life. This notion of justice is imperfect. Society does not tell us, for example, to steal from thieves. True sense of justice is administered with compassion and addresses the dignity of human beings and the sanctity of human life.

Even the families of victims of brutal murders sometimes advocate against the death penalty based on this principle. Despite the shock and anger they feel when a family member is killed, many survivors insist on valuing the sanctity of life above all else. Coretta Scott King, whose husband and mother-in-law were both murdered, is among those who maintain what some view as an _____ (CRED) statement: killers do not deserve the death penalty.

1. According to the essay, on what grounds do many people oppose the death penalty?
    A. They value the sanctity of life.
    B. The death penalty is fairly applied.
    C. The death penalty is costly.
    D. Murderers should pay with their lives.

2. What is the main point the author makes?
    A. Some survivors oppose the death penalty.
    B. The death penalty is wrong and should be eliminated.
    C. The death penalty is the ultimate justice.
    D. The death penalty is fair enough.

3. Which of the following would be the best title for the passage?
    A. An Introduction to the Death Penalty
    B. The Injustice of the Death Penalty
    C. Coretta Scott King's Opinion
    D. For or Against the Death Penalty

4. According to the author, why might the death penalty fail to deter murder?
    A. Citizens fail to see the horror of murder when the state permits death sentences.
    B. The worst criminals do not always receive death sentences.
    C. Citizens understand the healing power of forgiveness.
    D. Murder is already illegal.

Exercise VI. Drawing on your knowledge of roots and words in context, read the following selection and define the *italicized* words. If you cannot figure out the meaning of the words on your own, look them up in a dictionary. Note that *dis* means "apart," and *in* means "not."

The two priests have been involved in a religious *dispute* for many years. Although it started out as a friendly argument, it is now an ugly fight; the men exchange words over the phone, by email, and through the people who attend their churches. Each priest has accused the other of being an *infidel*, but neither can prove that the other has broken any laws of faith.

UNIT ELEVEN

MILITA
Latin MILITARE, MILITATUM, "to be a soldier"

MILITANT (mil´ ə tənt) *adj.* Willing to fight for a belief or cause; strongly
    devoted
Nasha is a *militant* supporter of women's rights; she is often in court defending
her cause.
syn: aggressive   *ant:* shy

MILITARIZE (mil´ ə tər īz) *v.* To prepare for war
During World War II, Congress avoided trying to *militarize* the general population, but many Civil Defense Units were ordered to serve in the army.

SOC
Latin SOCIUS, "ally, friend, comrade"
SOCIARE, SOCIATUM, "join, associate; have in common"

ASSOCIATE (ə sō´ shē āt) *v.* To link; to group together
L. ad, "to," + sociatum = *join to*
Anna refused to *associate* her eating with her poor health until a doctor
explained that she ate too much junk food.
syn: connect   *ant:* separate

SOCIALIZE (sō´ shə līz) *v.* To join in group activities
The president of the company never *socialized* with any of her employees.
syn: keep company   *ant:* avoid

SOCIABLE (sō´ shə bəl) *adj.* Interacting with others; friendly
We took our puppy to obedience school to try to get him to be more *sociable*
around other animals.
syn: outgoing   *ant:* isolated

ASOCIAL (ā´ sōsh əl) *adj.* Not enjoying or seeking the company of others
L. a, "not," + socius = *not a friend*
The new girl seemed *asocial* at first, but soon
her outgoing personality made her many
friends.
syn: unfriendly   *ant:* neighborly

One twin was WAY SOCIAL, the other ASOCIAL.

 Someone who is
militant *does not have to
be in an army or fighting
force. A militant sup-
porter of animal rights,
for instance, is someone
who strongly believes
animals should not be
treated cruelly and
shows that belief by
speaking, demonstrating,
contributing money, or
some other method.*

HOST
Latin HOSTIS, "enemy"

HOST   (hōst) *n.*   A large group; a great number
Terry's respiratory system was very weak, and a *host* of diseases began to attack her before she could be admitted to the hospital.
syn: crowd

HOSTILE   (hos´ təl)   *adj.*   Not friendly; warlike
The Lewis and Clark expedition encountered some *hostile* tribes, but most Native Americans the explorers met were friendly.
syn: unkind   *ant:* pleasant

COMPAN
Latin COMPANIS, "friend, associate"

COMPANIONSHIP   (kəm pan´ yən ship)   *n.*   Friendship; company
As odd as it may seem, Lou thought a robot dog would provide his lonely child with lots of *companionship*.

ACCOMPANIMENT   (ə kəm´ pən ē mənt)   *n.* Something that goes with
In Hannah's house, classical music was the usual *accompaniment* to dinner.

A host originally meant "a large number of enemy forces or troops, but now means simple "a great number." In modern English, if we say someone has a host of complaints, we mean that person seems to have an endless number of things to complain about.

Your companion is literally someone who shares bread ("panis") with ("com") you. This could be a partner, a close friend, or just someone who is with you for a short time.

EXERCISES - UNIT ELEVEN

Exercise I. Complete the sentence in a way that shows you understand the meaning of the italicized vocabulary word.

1. I enjoy the *companionship* of my dog Sparky because...

2. Gina was known as a *militant* patriot, and she often...

3. Brian had a *host* of friends, so he was often...

4. Liza seemed *asocial* when she did things like...

5. Ronald refused to *associate* with any of the other employees at the office because...

6. Because my mother is a very *sociable* person, she often...

7. The crowd seemed *hostile* towards the comedian, so she...

8. Many students come to the library to *socialize* rather than to...

9. The singer had the *accompaniment* of a piano so that he could...

10.   The country will be forced to *militarize* its borders if...

Exercise II. Fill in the blank with the best word from the choices below. One word will not be used.

militant   companionship   asocial   host

1.   After his girlfriend broke up with him, Dirk became completely _____ and stopped going out at all.

2.   When the police ended the protest march, a group of the more _____ marchers began to riot.

3.   Oliver was lonely and looking for _____ when he met his future wife.

Fill in the blank with the best word from the choices below. One word will not be used.

sociable   hostile   associates   militarizes

4. Tamara didn't like Charles very much, but she tried not to act _____ toward him.

5. Because my sister _____ with a lot of artists, she knows quite a bit about painting and sculpture.

6. Charlie urged his little brother to be _____ and friendly at the birthday party.

Fill in the blank with the best word from the choices below. One word will not be used.

militarized   companionship   socialize   accompaniment   host

7. After the war, areas that had been _____ were given back to the civilians by the soldiers.

8. Although Marie is very shy, she will _____ freely with her friends and family.

9. The manager needs to replace a(n) _____ of non-working machines in the factory before the place is in shape to open.

10. It was difficult to work to the _____ of car horns and jackhammers.

Exercise III. Choose the set of words that best completes the sentence.

1. Once the town had been _____, soldiers from the two camps were no longer allowed to _____ with one another.
    A. associated; militarize
    B. militarized; associate
    C. hosted; associate
    D. accompanied; socialize

2. Because Danny was a(n) _____ supporter of his favorite hockey team, he spent most of his time at home watching their games and gained a reputation for being _____.
    A. militant; sociable
    B. asocial; sociable
    C. sociable; militant
    D. militant; asocial

3. Although Inez, the famous singer, had a(n) _____ of admiring fans at her door every night, she longed for the _____ of a true friend.
    A. host; companionship
    B. companionship; associate
    C. companionship; host
    D. accompaniment; host

4. I could tell that Greg and Grace were fighting because they acted _____ and would not _____ with each other.
    A. asocial; militarize
    B. hostile; associate
    C. sociable; accompany
    D. militant; associate

5. The wine was a fine _____ to the meal, and, along with our _____ hostess, made for a very pleasant evening.
    A. accompaniment; sociable
    B. companionship; asocial
    C. companionship; hostile
    D. accompaniment; militant

Exercise IV. Complete the sentence by inferring information about the italicized word from its context.

1. In order to prove he is *sociable*, Doug might…

2. If a pet can provide an elderly person with some *companionship*, it probably means…

3. Because Monique doesn't *associate* with her sister much any more, their friends might assume…

Exercise V. Fill in the blank with the word from the Unit that best completes the sentence, using the root we supply as a clue. Then, answer the questions that follow the paragraphs.

Should students wear uniforms to school? Some United States public schools are requiring their students to wear them because of the supposed educational advantages. Others believe that school uniform requirements stifle creativity and violate the First Amendment, which guarantees freedom of expression.

Supporters of school uniforms say that above all, sameness in clothing eliminates a major visual distraction to students. This can provide a _____(HOST) of secondary benefits. Students who might use clothing to make political statements or show gang colors are prevented from doing so when uniform requirements are in place. In addition, uniforms help schools circumvent any problems with obscene or revealing clothing. And uniforms help foster a sense of unity within the school, much as they do within the military.

On the other hand, both parents and students have argued that forcing students to look like one another can damage their sense of individuality and stifle original thinking. They _____(SOC) uniforms with dictators and tyrannical governments who brutally punished freedom of speech and thought. They also point out that uniforms cost money—money that either the school systems or the students' families must provide.

Meanwhile, members of religious groups worry that eliminating individualized clothing and accessories will mean prohibiting religious symbols that can be important to students, as in France, where no outward sign of a student's religion—including yarmulkes for Jewish students and headscarves for Muslim girls—may be worn in a public school.

The arguments for and against school uniforms both have sound reasoning—and many supporters—behind them. A solution that satisfies both parties may be possible, in fact: a uniform requirement that takes religious preference, financial difficulties, and freedom of choice into account. Under this system, students would wear uniforms, but be allowed to express their religious or political beliefs through accessories. Families unable to pay would receive aid from the school district. And students strongly opposed to the uniforms would be allowed not to wear them. Perhaps this arrangement would allow schools to reap the benefits of school uniforms without violating any student's freedom.

1. The best title for this passage would be
    A. "The School Uniform Debate."
    B. "Teachers Encourage Dress Codes."
    C. "Students Don't Like Uniforms."
    D. "Dress Codes and No Uniforms."

2. The word "circumvent" in the second paragraph means
    A. show.
    B. promise.
    C. admire.
    D. avoid.

3. The author of this passage seems to think that
    A. arguments for and against uniforms make sense.
    B. school uniforms are required.
    C. the financial cost of uniforms is too high.
    D. the First Amendment is violated by uniform requirements.

4. The purpose of this passage is to
    A. convince the reader that school uniforms are necessary.
    B. explain the history of school uniforms.
    C. describe the problems faced by students wearing uniforms in France.
    D. present both sides of the school uniform debate.

Exercise VI. Drawing on your knowledge of roots and words in context, read the following selection and define the *italicized* words. If you cannot figure out the meaning of the words on your own, look them up in a dictionary. Note that *dis* means "away."

When Mari decided that she needed to spend more time studying, she tried to *dissociate* herself from her group of noisy, party-loving friends. She politely turned down invitations to parties, and when the group went out to dinner, she stayed home. When asked, she said that they had been her friends, but were not now. For their part, these friends no longer found her *companionable*; they even started calling her "Mean Mari."

UNIT TWELVE

CAPITA
Latin CAPUT, CAPITIS, "head"

CAPITALIZE　(kap´ ə təl īz)　v.　To make the best of
The star athlete wanted to *capitalize* on her fame and quickly signed a deal to appear in TV commercials.
syn: take advantage of　　　　　*ant*: miss out on

DECAPITATE　(dē kap´ ə tāt)　v.　To remove the head of
Police officers were shocked when the captain said he wanted to *decapitate* the gang, but he explained that he meant to separate the leader from the members.
syn: behead

ORA
Latin OS, ORIS, "mouth"

ORAL　(ôr´ əl)　*adj.*　1. Having to do with the mouth
　　　　　　　　　　　　2. Spoken, rather than written
1. The dentist told Helene that without better *oral* care, she would need mouth surgery within a year.
2. The myths of the tribe were passed down through an *oral* tradition.

ORATORY　(ôr´ ə tôr ē)　*n.*　The art of public speaking
When he was in college, *oratory* was our teacher's favorite subject; he certainly does lecture a lot in class.

ORATION　(ôr ā´ shən)　*n.*　A grand, formal speech
Jim's *oration* was boring, and only a few students voted for him after the speech.
syn: recitation

The words of his ORATION rang out across the NATION.

The Latin "capitis" has given us English words with a variety of meanings. For instance, capital can describe an uppercase letter, a city that is the center of government, or an amount of money. All of these things are at the head or beginning of something.

You may hear decapitate used to mean "behead a person," but it can also mean "to ruin an organization or system." For instance, if someone says a power outage decapitated a city's government, we know that the government was unable to function until the power came back on.

MAN, MANU
Latin MANUS, "hand"

MANUFACTURE (man ū fak´ shər) *v.* To build; to make
L. manus, "hand," + facere = *to make by hand*
John is the manager of a company that *manufactures* toothbrushes.

MANUAL (man´ ū əl) *adj.* Done by hand
Manual operation of the pump became necessary when the power went out.

EMANCIPATE (ē man´ sə pāt) *v.* To set free
L. e, "out of," + manceps, "one who takes with the hand, slaveowner" = *out of slavery*
A trespasser was killed when he broke into the zoo and tried to *emancipate* the tigers.
syn: liberate   *ant*: imprison

LING
Latin LINGUA, "tongue"

MULTILINGUAL (mul tē ling´ wəl) *adj.* Speaking several languages
L. multus, "many," + lingua = *many tongues*
Before her trip to Europe, Danielle received a *multilingual* dictionary.

LINGUISTIC (lin gwis´ tək) *adj.* Having to do with the structure of language
The police do not know who left the threatening message on my answering machine, but they are doing a *linguistic* analysis to find clues.

▤ Like the word manuscript, manufacture *no longer means only "to make by hand." In fact, strangely enough, when people speak of manufacturing these days, they usually mean "building or producing something with machines."*

▤ *The Latin word "manceps," which originally came from "manus," means "one who leads by the hand," or "one who owns a slave." To be emancipated (e, "out of," + manceps, "slaveowner") is to be let out of slavery. One of the most famous uses of the word is in an important document of United States history. The Emancipation Proclamation, sent out by President Lincoln in 1863, freed all slaves in the United States.*

▤ *The science of linguistics is concerned with the way we speak and understand language, and the way language changes over time.*

EXERCISES - UNIT TWELVE

Exercise I. Complete the sentence in a way that shows you understand the meaning of the italicized vocabulary word.

1.   In order to *capitalize* on the good weather this year, the farmers…

2.   The rubber company has a license to *manufacture* things like…

3.   Because she came from a *multilingual* family, Rose…

4.   We studied the *linguistic* features of Spanish in order to…

5.   Pam had to take an *oral* Japanese examination, so she practiced…

6   When the low-flying helicopter *decapitated* the statue…

7.   The Senator's *oration* made everyone in the audience…

8.   None of the students liked the classroom's *manual* pencil sharpener because…

9.   The prisoners on the island hoped they would be *emancipated* by…

10. In order to understand the art of *oratory*, you have to know things like…

Exercise II. Fill in the blank with the best word from the choices below. One word will not be used.

oration   manual   multilingual   manufacture

1.   Once Craig had his shop in working order, he was able to _____ several hundred small clay statues a day.

2.   The members of the audience were so moved by the President's _____ that they stood up and applauded.

3.   The instructional video, which has Spanish, French, and Chinese subtitles, was made for a(n) _____ audience.

Fill in the blank with the best word from the choices below. One word will not be used.

oral   manual   linguistic   multilingual

4.   Researchers are studying the _____ patterns of babies to find out how we learn to talk.

5.   Many of the country's myths were not written down, but remained in _____ form.

6.   When the surgeon's complicated instrument stopped working, he had to use a(n) _____ technique in which he held the patient's heart still with his fingertips.

Fill in the blank with the best word from the choices below. One word will not be used.

decapitates   capitalize   emancipated   oratory   manual

7.   The wasp first _____ the caterpillar, then devours the headless body.

8.   Schoolboys in ancient Rome studied _____ in preparation for the speeches they would someday make.

9.   Once they had been _____ from their cruel master, the former servants headed for the city.

10.   Because Sarah did not _____ on her tax refund, she has very little money this year.

Exercise III. Choose the set of words that best completes the sentence.

1.   Joey decided to _____ on his _____ knowledge by taking a job in language study.
        A. decapitate; oral
        B. capitalize; linguistic
        C. manufacture; multilingual
        D. emancipate; linguistic

2.   Teresa was _____, having grown up in France, Japan, and England, and she could easily pass _____ and written exams in various languages.
        A. linguistic; oral
        B. multilingual; oral
        C. oral; manual
        D. manual; oral

3.   The _____ farm tool was easier to use than the electric one, but it was also more dangerous; if handled the wrong way, it could _____ a person.
        A. multilingual; decapitate
        B. linguistic; emancipate
        C. oral; manufacture
        D. manual; decapitate

4.   Some colleges focus on subjects like writing, _____ and acting, while other schools teach students how to _____ and sell products for profit.
     A. linguistics; emancipate
     B. oratory; manufacture
     C. capitalization; decapitate
     D. oratory; decapitate

5.   In his very powerful and emotional _____, the reverend said that all people should be _____ from the bonds of injustice.
     A. oration; emancipated
     B. linguistics; decapitated
     C. decapitation; manufactured
     D. oration; manufactured

Exercise IV. Complete the sentence by inferring information about the italicized word from its context.

1.   If the bicycle mechanic pointed out a *malfunction* in the brakes on your bike, your likely response would be to…

2.   A quick review of the *linguistic* study might help Arthur if he…

3.   If Henri decides to *capitalize* on his family's good reputation in the community, he may do thing like…

Exercise V. Fill in the blank with the word from the Unit that best completes the sentence, using the root we supply as a clue. Then, answer the questions that follow the paragraphs.

Although we often take for granted that we know how to read, reading is a great gift, one that Frederick Douglass did not come by easily. He was a slave who struggled hard to learn, and one who was rewarded greatly for his efforts. He is known as one of the greatest speakers in America's history. His _____ (ORA) were widely praised both in America and Europe for their wisdom and brilliance. Through his words, he not only freed himself, but also influenced the President who would one day free all the slaves.

When he was six years old, Frederick Douglass' first teacher was his owner's wife. However, when she told her husband she had taught Frederick the alphabet and a few simple words, the man became furious and ordered her to stop. Her husband told her it was unlawful to teach slaves to read because then they might start to think and no longer obey unquestioningly. Worse, they might obtain the ability to forge papers indicating that they were free; this would have been an easy way to escape to the North, where slavery was outlawed. Frederick overheard his master's arguments and immediately decided he must learn to read and write in order to become free.

He knew he could learn from the poor white children he met when he was sent on errands, so he saved pieces of bread and used them to pay for lessons. At home, he tried to sneak his reading in whenever he could, catching bits and pieces from books or newspapers that were lying about. Eventually Frederick was able to have a book of his own. With the little money he made from doing errands, he finally saved up enough to buy *The Columbian Orator*, a book of speeches and essays about democracy, freedom, and courage. Frederick then began to read local newspapers, where he learned about abolitionists, men and women who were trying to put an end to slavery. At thirteen years old, he was already determined not only to free himself, but to do what he could to help _____ (MAN) other slaves.

Frederick continued to learn, and by the time he was sixteen, he had started an illegal school for blacks. He was also admitted to an educational association formed by free blacks, where he learned debating skills. At twenty, he finally escaped to the North, where he started reading a newspaper called the *Liberator*. "The paper became my meat and drink," he wrote. "My soul was set on fire." Douglass eventually became an outstanding speaker for the anti-slavery movement. He told people the facts about the cruelties of slavery, of slaves being beaten and families being broken up. He finally became an advisor and close friend of Abraham Lincoln himself. To this day Frederick Douglass stands on a pedestal in American history. It is a stand he built himself, not brick by brick, but letter by letter, word by word.

1. The best title for this essay would be
   A. "Fight for your Beliefs."
   B. "Believe in the Power of Words."
   C. "Frederick Douglass: What Words Can Do."
   D. "Slavery: The Struggle to Abolish It."

2. Once Frederick Douglass got to the North,
   A. he became inspired by a newspaper called the *Liberator*.
   B. he became a speaker for the antislavery movement.
   C. he influenced Abraham Lincoln.
   D. All of the above

3. The essay explains that
   A. reading was unlawful for slaves.
   B. Frederick Douglass wanted to get back at his master for not letting him read.
   C. Frederick Douglass thought his mistress should have continued teaching him.
   D. All of the above

4. This essay illustrates that
   A. education is priceless.
   B. trouble in life can spur a person on to greater things.
   C. things take time.
   D. All of the above

Exercise VI. Drawing on your knowledge of roots and words in context, read the following selection and define the *italicized* words. If you cannot figure out the meaning of the words on your own, look them up in a dictionary. Note that *mission* means "sent, released."

The sailors in the ship's prison hoped and prayed for *manumission*, but remained locked up until the ship reached a port in Egypt. While they were in prison, which in sailors' *lingo* is called "the brig," they passed the time by playing cards, singing songs, and sleeping. These things were difficult, though, because the jail was very small, and there was not much food or water.

UNIT THIRTEEN

JUBIL
Latin JUBILARE, JUBILATUM, "to shout for joy"

JUBILEE (jōō bə lē´) *n.* A joyous celebration
The town held a giant *jubilee* to celebrate the opening of the new store that would employ a hundred residents and bring in a great deal of money.
syn: party

JUBILANT (jōō´ bə lənt) *adj.* Full of joy
When Trina found out that she had graduated with the highest average in her class, she was *jubilant.*
syn: merry, delighted   *ant:* sad

HILAR
Latin HILARIS, "cheerful"

HILARITY (hə la´ rə tē) *n.* Fun; merriment
The sequel is funny, but it does not match the crazy *hilarity* of the first movie.
syn: glee   *ant:* sadness

EXHILARATING (eks zil´ ə rāt ing) *adj.* Bringing great joy and excitement
L. ex, "very," + hilaris = *to make very cheerful*
Georgina was terrified of heights, but she felt skydiving would be *exhilarating.*
syn: stimulating   *ant:* disappointing

FRUG, FRUI
Latin FRUI, FRUCTUS, "to enjoy"

FRUITFUL (frōōt´ fəl) *adj.* Bringing forth much; productive
The weather was perfect this summer, and we had a *fruitful* harvest of tomatoes.
syn: rich   *ant:* barren

FRUGAL (frōō´ gəl) *adj.* Not spending much money; cheap
If Murray's mother hadn't been so *frugal* when he was young, the family never could have afforded to send him to medical school.
syn: thrifty   *ant:* wasteful

The FRUGAL BUGLER bought all his trumpets at a yard sale.

CELEBER, CELEBR
Latin CELEBRARE, CELEBRATUM, " to celebrate, honor"

CELEBRATORY (sel´ ə brə tôr ē)   *adj.* Of or relating to a party or ceremony
Sue sent out *celebratory* notices announcing the marriage of her daughter.
syn: festive

CELEBRANT (sel´ ə brənt)   *n.* One who takes part in a ceremony, especially a
   religious ceremony
One of the *celebrants* in the worship service almost dropped her candle.

CELEBRITY (se leb´ ri tē) *n.* Recognition by many; fame
Mort achieved his *celebrity* for all the right reasons; the papers praised his charity,
good deeds, and interest in helping the homeless.
syn: stardom   *ant:* anonymity

LUD, LUS
Latin LUDUS, "game"
LUDERE, LUSUM, "to play"

ILLUSION (ə lōō´ shən)   *n.*   A false image or idea
L. in, "on, against," + ludere = *play on*
Achara thought that she saw a lake in the distance, but it turned out to be an
illusion.
syn: trick   *ant:* reality

DELUDE (də lōōd´) *v.*   To trick; to fool
L. de, "away from," + ludere = *to play away from*
Cigarette smokers often *delude* themselves into believing that they will not be
affected by the diseases smoking causes.
syn: cheat   *ant:* be truthful

EXERCISES - UNIT THIRTEEN

Exercise I. Complete the sentence in a way that shows you understand the meaning of the italicized vocabulary word.

1. The pumpkin crop was so *fruitful* this year that…

2. The children in the circus audience were *jubilant* because…

3. Stanley wished that he had been more *frugal* when…

4. The hot dog salesman was able to *delude* his customers by saying that…

5. The residents of Trentville decided to have a *jubilee* when…

6. Bungee jumping was an *exhilarating* experience because…

7. On the last day of the year, everyone was in a *celebratory* mood because…

8. The hypnotist made a member of the audience believe she was a *celebrant* in…

9. The tennis player, who had once been unknown, gained much *celebrity* when…

10.   Hannah's wedding was a day of great *hilarity* because…

11.   Nina was under the *illusion* that Santa Claus existed until…

Exercise II. Fill in the blank with the best word from the choices below. One word will not be used.

   illusion   celebratory   jubilee   delude   frugal

1.   When we heard on the radio that the war had ended, we rushed out into the street and had a(n) _____.

2.   We could tell by the balloons and streamers hung in our office that our boss was in a(n) _____ mood.

3.   The magician depended on _____ to convince his audience that the scarf had disappeared.

4.   Jeremy tried to _____ his sister into thinking there was no more cake.

Fill in the blank with the best word from the choices below. One word will not be used.

celebratory   celebrant   hilarity   jubilant   frugal

5. The great comedians always manage to bring _____ to the stage, even in very serious times.

6. My grandparents are _____ people who rarely buy new clothes or furniture.

7. Derek's _____ expression let us know he had passed his test with flying colors.

8. Father Conley, who is now head priest, was once a minor _____ in the weekly Church service.

Fill in the blank with the best word from the choices below. One word will not be used.

fruitful   celebratory   celebrity   exhilarating

9. The _____ of Muhammad Ali was so great that he was known even in tiny, faraway villages.

10. As a new pilot, George found every flight _____ and delightful.

11. Our brainstorming session was so _____ that we filled up forty pages with new ideas.

Exercise III. Choose the set of words that best completes the sentence.

1. Though my birthday _____ started out on a sad note, sounds of joy and _____ soon filled the air.
   A. celebrity; illusion
   B. hilarity; illusion
   C. illusion; celebrity
   D. jubilee; hilarity

2. Despite the _____ of the pianist, the citizens in the small town had never heard of her; nonetheless, they found her music amazing and _____.
   A. celebrity; exhilarating
   B. hilarity; frugal
   C. hilarity; celebratory
   D. illusion; exhilarating

3. Because Omar was under the _____ that he was going bankrupt, he became very _____ when he went shopping.
   A. celebrant; fruitful
   B. illusion; jubilant
   C. hilarity; fruitful
   D. illusion; frugal

4. Although the volunteers' efforts to clean up the river have been _____, they should not _____ themselves into thinking all the problems have been solved.
    A. fruitful; delude
    B. jubilant; exhilarate
    C. celebratory; delude
    D. frugal; exhilarate

5. The _____ mood of the crowd after the home team won was clear from the _____ expressions on their faces.
    A. exhilarating; frugal
    B. jubilant; frugal
    C. fruitful; jubilant
    D. celebratory; jubilant

Exercise IV. Complete the sentence by inferring information about the italicized word from its context.

1. If the results of Jorge's job search were *fruitful*, we could expect…

2. If the ghost is not an *illusion*, Hillary will probably…

3. Because everyone at the party was in a *jubilant* mood, Marcie…

Exercise V. Fill in the blank with the word from the Unit that best completes the sentence, using the root we supply as a clue. Then, answer the questions that follow the paragraphs.

Muslims in South Africa may give the _____(LUS) of being a homogenous group, but they make up a very complex mixed community of people. They include descendants of people from India, Bali, and Indonesia, as well as those originating in South Africa. South African Islam reflects the particular history and politics of this area as well as the cultural differences between each group.

Around 1654, Dutch ships began bringing people to South Africa from colonies in India, Indonesia, Sri Lanka, and surrounding areas. Some were slaves or indentured servants; others were political dissidents who had opposed the Dutch government. These were the people who would eventually become known as the "Cape Malay" (from their supposed origins in Malaysia) or the "Cape Muslims"—the first Muslims in South Africa. They built mosques and other holy sites, and were among the first speakers of *Afrikaans*—a version of Dutch that is still spoken in South Africa today. During *apartheid* (the system of racial segregation that was in place until the 1990s), the Cape Muslims were categorized as "coloured"; this meant that they had fewer rights and educational opportunities than white South Africans, although they still had more opportunities than their black neighbors.

In the 1990s, after years of struggle, apartheid was legally abolished. During this _____(JUB) period, free and democratic elections were held for the first time in South Africa, and groups of all races were permitted to interact freely. At this time, Islam began to grow in popularity among black South Africans. Many of them see conversion to Islam as an escape from a dangerous, hopeless existence. They say they like Islam's focus on charity (one of the five pillars of Islam is giving to the needy). They also like the structure and discipline of Islam; in areas where drug abuse and AIDS kill many young people, a religion that stresses clean living can be seen as a way out. Black Africans are now the fastest-growing segment of the Muslim population in modern South Africa.

There is ongoing tension between black South African Muslims and those of different racial and historical backgrounds, as well as between Muslims and Christians (about seventy percent of South Africa's population is Christian). As South Africa's democracy develops, however, the Muslim community will likely become stronger and more unified, and also continue to grow.

1. The first Muslims in South Africa were primarily
    A. young people trying to escape crime and poverty.
    B. people from Indonesia, India, and Sri Lanka.
    C. musicians who wrote holy songs.
    D. Dutch traders.

2. From the passage, the word *dissident* probably means
    A. a person who disagrees with a ruling party or government.
    B. a person who lives in a country.
    C. a slave or indentured servant.
    D. a king or queen.

3. According to the passage, young South Africans are converting to Islam because
    A. they are a fast-growing segment of the population.
    B. they wish to be more like the Cape Muslims.
    C. they see it as a way out of poverty and hopelessness.
    D. there is tension between Muslims and Christians.

4. Compared to white South Africans, the Cape Muslim population
    A. had fewer rights.
    B. had more education.
    C. had more freedom.
    D. had more opportunities.

Exercise VI. Drawing on your knowledge of roots and words in context, read the following selection and define the *italicized* words. If you cannot figure out the meaning of the words on your own, look them up in a dictionary. Note that *al*, from *ad*, means "towards," and *–vore* means "eating."

In her article, Professor Harling spends a lot of time writing about environmental problems that have hurt the gorilla population. Although she never comes out and directly criticizes the governments responsible for these problems, she does *allude* to disasters caused by government neglect. For instance, she says that many fruit trees have been cut down to make room for houses. For *frugivores* like gorillas, this can lead to starvation.

UNIT FOURTEEN

PLIC, PLEX

Latin PLECTERE, PLEXUS, "to weave"
PLICARE, PLICATUM, "to fold"

APPLICATION   (a pli kā´ shən)   *n.*   1. Use
                                                   2. Putting on
L. ad, "towards, onto" + plicatum = *to fold onto*
1. There seemd to be no *application* for the tool the inventor designed.
2. An *application* of the cream to the rash should provide relief in a few days.

COMPLEX   (kom pleks´)   *adj.*   complicated
L. com, "together," + plexus = *woven together, complicated*
Kenny's *complex* math problem was so hard that even his father couldn't figure out the answer.
syn: intricate   *ant:* easy

DUPLICATE   (dōōp´ lə kāt)   *v.*   To make another; to copy
Because the job was detailed and difficult, the manager made sure the two people involved *duplicated* each other's work.
syn: reproduce

TEXT

Latin TEXERE, TEXTUS, "to weave"

TEXTURE   (tekst´ shər)   *n.*   The way something feels to the touch
The soft *texture* of the blanket was comforting to the baby.

TEXTILE   (teks´ tīl)   *n.*   Cloth or fabric
In the ancient culture, people wove beautiful *textiles* into rugs, hanging decorations, and blankets.

▥ *Complex is a word that has various meanings: it means complicated, as in a complex job; it means made up of parts, as in an apartment complex; it means a mental influence on behavior, as in an inferiority complex; it is used in grammar, as in a complex sentence, or with math, as in a complex fraction. All these uses, though, imply the original meaning of more than one thing woven or folded together.*

VEAL, VEIL
Latin VELARE, VELATUM, "to cover"

REVEAL (rē vēl´) *v.* To make known
L. re, "back," + velare = *to pull the cover back*
You should never *reveal* your Social Security Number on the phone.
syn: show   *ant*: hide

UNVEIL (un vāl´) *v.* To uncover
The name of the latest person to win the multimillion-dollar prize will be *unveiled* on national television next week.

MANTL
Latin MANTELLUM, "cloak"

MANTLED (man´ təld) *adj.* Covered; draped
Latitia lived in a home that was *mantled* in beautiful green ivy.

DISMANTLE (dis man´ təl) *v.* To take apart
L. dis, "apart," + mantellum = to take off a cloak, remove walls, destroy
All Harriet's efforts to *dismantle* the security alarm failed, and she had to call the company for help.
syn: break down   *ant*: construct

The VANDAL DISMANTLED the statue.

▥ *The words* mantle *and* dismantle *came through French before English got them. The French "mantel" meant about the same thing that our English* mantle *does; "desmanteler," from which we get* dismantle, *actually meant "to destroy a town's defenses, knock down its walls." So, from the idea of taking off a cloak, to removing a town's defenses, to taking something completely apart, this word has had a long journey.*

EXERCISES - UNIT FOURTEEN

Exercise I. Complete the sentence in a way that shows you understand the meaning of the italicized vocabulary word.

1.   During the month of January, our farm is usually *mantled* in…

2.   When Jan tried to *duplicate* the original document, she found that…

3.   Benito will *reveal* the secret to the puzzle so we can…

4.   When the mayor *unveiled* the new statue, the crowd…

5.   The *texture* of the silk shirt reminded Jeffrey of…

6.   The math problem was more *complex* than we had thought, so we…

7.   More than one *application* of paint was required for the wall because…

8.   The workers at the garage had to *dismantle* the car's engine in order to…

9.   The country's main export was *textiles*, which could be used for things like…

Exercise II. Fill in the blank with the best word from the choices below. One word will not be used.

> unveil   duplicate   mantled   application

1.   The painting was so amazing that no one could ever _____ it, although many people tried.

2.   An oven mitt can have more than one _____, as Angelo discovered when he lost his baseball glove.

3.   The glamorous actress was _____ in furs and silks on the film's opening night.

Fill in the blank with the best word from the choices below. One word will not be used.

> textiles   unveiled   dismantled

4.   When the author _____ the true identity of the famous singer, everyone was stunned.

5.   Cotton was important for making _____ in the pre-War South.

Fill in the blank with the best word from the choices below. One word will not be used.

       dismantled   texture   reveal   complex   mantled

6.   Although the physics project had many _____ steps, Nicki was able to complete it with ease.

7.   The carpenter felt the _____ of the chair to make sure it was smooth enough.

8.   Kylie completely _____ her doll in order to see how the inside worked.

9.   No matter how I beg my best friend, she will not _____ the name of my secret admirer.

Exercise III. Choose the set of words that best completes the sentence.

1.   The _____ of the animal's fur is so unique and so delicate that it cannot be _____ by scientists.
     A. texture; mantled
     B. textile; dismantled
     C. texture; duplicated
     D. textile; mantled

2.   The medical handbook suggests the _____ of a bandage, made of cotton or a similar _____, to the wound.
     A. application; textile
     B. textile; texture
     C. application; texture
     D. textile; application

3.   Though the project at the space lab has been _____ in secrecy, there are rumors that the plans for it will be _____ today.
     A. duplicated; unveiled
     B. mantled; unveiled
     C. revealed; duplicated
     D. unveiled; mantled

4.   The dinosaur skeleton was so _____ that it took the museum employees hours to _____ and move it.
     A. mantled; reveal
     B. complex; dismantle
     C. mantled; duplicate
     D. complex; reveal

Exercise IV. Complete the sentence by inferring information about the italicized word from its context.

1. Since the *texture* of the shirt made him itch, Dylan…

2. If Norman's parents *dismantle* his beloved tree house, Norman will probably…

3. During the game, if Gregg doesn't want to *reveal* his hiding place, he might…

Exercise V. Fill in the blank with the word from the Unit that best completes the sentence, using the root we supply as a clue. Then, answer the questions that follow the paragraphs.

Model railroading is a time-honored hobby meant to _____ (VEAL) a person's artistic ability as well as fulfill a God-like desire to create a world in miniature. When most people think of model railroading, they remember having a train run under the Christmas tree and then putting it away until the following holiday. Serious, dedicated railroaders, however, build _____ (PLEX) sets in their basements or garages that stay up year round, often _____ (PLIC) an actual city or townscape, complete with realistic looking buildings, mountains, grass, trees, and waterways.

Those interested in model railroading must decide how much time and money they are willing to invest in the hobby because layouts can be made cheaply without looking cheap, or they can be very expensive. The first major purchases are the trains, which come in a variety of scales, from the tiny N scale to the large G; the most popular scale is called HO. After purchasing the train and all the track necessary, some people also buy fake trees and plastic buildings, while others prefer to build everything themselves by hand.

The first major piece of construction is the platform that will hold the miniature world. It pays to have some carpentry experience because platforms are not on sale at the local hardware store. Sheets of plywood, laid horizontally, are best for the surface. However, most people don't like working on the floor, so the model railroader will build a system of legs and crossbeams to support the plywood, usually at a height of four feet. It must be level; most model trains cannot function with more than a three-degree slope.

Once the platform is ready, the railroader must decide where the track will be laid and whether the model landscape will be fictional or based on an actual place. Many railroaders find it more challenging to duplicate an actual urban business district with miniature skyscrapers embossed with the names of actual corporations, while others prefer to build rural landscapes of farms, fields and woodlands. It's the builder's world, and it's up to that person to decide how it should look.

Once a course of action is decided upon, artistry is next, with the surface of the plywood as the canvas. The track is put in its desired route, along with buildings, trees, mountains, etc.; the layout then becomes a three-dimensional and functional work of art.

The _____ (VEIL) of the masterpiece to family and friends is the next-to-last step. The real reward comes when the builder becomes enveloped in the "oohs" and "aahs" of observers as the electricity is turned on and everyone is impressed.

1. Why is the platform most important to a model layout?
   A. The railroader must have a solid, level place to build the environment.
   B. It's not important at all.
   C. The railroader wants to construct the environment on the floor.
   D. Both A and C

2. Why would people be interested in model railroading, according to the passage?
   A. It's a form of artistic expression.
   B. They have an interest in trains.
   C. They like to be creative.
   D. All of the above

3. What is the most popular scale in model railroading?
   A. HO
   B. N
   C. G
   D. D

4. Why does the author feel it is more challenging to reconstruct an actual landscape?
   A. Fictional places must be to scale.
   B. Factual places are easily copied.
   C. People know a real place and will quickly notice anything wrong.
   D. The author does not say.

Exercise VI. Drawing on your knowledge of roots and words in context, read the following selection and define the *italicized* words. If you cannot figure out the meaning of the words on your own, look them up in a dictionary. Note that *per* means "through."

The gardener was *perplexed* by the death of many flowers in the garden. He had given the plants plenty of water, air and sunlight, so he could not understand why they would not grow. After thinking about this problem for a long time, he had a *revelation*: he realized that the flowers had a rare disease caused by a kind of mold. When this thought came to him, he jumped up and shouted, "Of course! That's it!"

UNIT FIFTEEN

SEQ, SEC
Latin SEQUI, SECUTUS, "to follow"

SEQUEL (sē´ kwəl) *n.* Something, especially a work of art or literature, that
    follows an original
Grace went to see every *sequel* of the outer space series about life on Mars.

SEQUENCE (sē´ kwens) *n.* The order in which something happens
Todd forgot the *sequence* of battles in the Civil War, so his grade went from an *A*
to a *C*.

PROSECUTE (pro´ sə kūt) *v.* To press charges against
L. pro, "forth, forward" + secutus = *to follow forward*
The District Attorney wanted to *prosecute* him for robbery, but there wasn't
enough evidence.
syn: try (as in a trial)

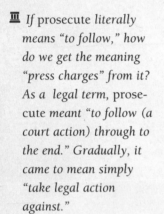

If you SHOOT, I'll PROSECUTE!

▥ *If prosecute literally
means "to follow," how
do we get the meaning
"press charges" from it?
As a legal term, prose-
cute meant "to follow (a
court action) through to
the end." Gradually, it
came to mean simply
"take legal action
against."*

DUCT, DUCE
Latin DUCERE, DUCTUS, "to lead"

CONDUCT (kən dukt´) *v.* To lead; to oversee
L. con, "together," + ductum = *to lead together*
As the captain of the hockey team, Michael had to *conduct* afternoon practice.
syn: govern; run

PRODUCE (prə dōōs´) *v.* To bring forth; create
L. pro, "forth," + ducere = *to lead forth*
Detroit *produces* more cars than any other place in the United States.
syn: make

ABDUCT (ab dukt´) *v.* To kidnap
L. ab, "away from," + ductum = *to lead away from*
The childless couple was charged with trying to *abduct* a little boy from his
natural parents.
syn: steal

VEH, VECT
Latin VEHERE, VECTUS, "to carry"

VEHICLE (vē´ ik əl) *n.* Something that carries
In 1900, gasoline-powered *vehicles* were almost never seen.

CONVECTION (kən vek´ shən) *n.* The movement of heat in a gas or liquid
L. con, "together," + vectus = *to carry together*
Mirages are common in the desert because the hot air rises, and this *convection* causes false images to appear.

TRACT
Latin TRAHERE, TRACTUS, "to draw, drag"

ATTRACTIVE (ə trak´ tiv) *adj.* Pleasing
L. ad, "towards," + tractus = *drawing towards*
The nearness of the house to her workplace was one thing that made it *attractive* to Beth.
syn: appealing   *ant*: unpleasant

CONTRACT (kən trakt´) *v.* To draw together; tighten
L. con, "together," + tractus = *draw together*
Water is the only substance that expands when it freezes; everything else *contracts*.
syn: squeeze   *ant*: widen; enlarge

DISTRACT (dis trakt´) *v.* To take someone's attention away
L. dis, "apart, away" + tractus = *draw away*
Liz was trying to read, but nearly everyone in the office was *distracting* her.
syn: draw away   *ant*: captivate

Ⅲ Vehicle *is most often used to mean "a form of motorized transportation." It can also mean "something which serves or carries an idea or goal." For instance, if a movie is clearly made only so that the movie star can look pretty in it, we might say the movie is a good* vehicle *for her.*

Ⅲ *The best way to remember* convection *is to think of a pot boiling on a stove. Because heat rises, warmer water moves to the top surface of the pot. There, because it is not as close to the stove as before, it cools down, sinks, and the process begins*

EXERCISES - UNIT FIFTEEN

Exercise I. Complete the sentence in a way that shows you understand the meaning of the italicized vocabulary word.

1.   The hospital uses brightly-colored toys to *distract* children who are…

2.   Because the town badly needed a *vehicle* to use as an ambulance, it…

3.   The district attorney will *prosecute* Ann if…

4.   Nadine found the idea of a job in the circus very *attractive* because…

5.   When asked to *produce* an important document, Dave said that he…

6.   The two bank employees plan to *abduct* their boss so they…

7.   The *sequence* of events in Dylan's story was out of order because…

8.   Because the oven worked by *convection*, the heat in it…

9.   Our manager will *conduct* the meeting in a way that is…

10. Though the eye doctor expected the patient's pupils to *contract*, they actually…

11. Mr. Yamaguchi decided to write a *sequel* to his novel so that…

Exercise II. Fill in the blank with the best word from the choices below. One word will not be used.

conducted   produce   sequence   attractive   prosecute

1.   There was no way we could _____ all of the paintings in time for the gallery exhibition.

2.   The students had to watch their teacher closely to learn the difficult _____ of dance steps.

3.   The dress is certainly very _____, but not worth the high price being asked.

4.   Jonathan's teacher praised him for the way he _____ the meeting.

Fill in the blank with the best word from the choices below. One word will not be used.

sequel   vehicle   sequence   contract   abducted

5. Everyone agreed that the _____ to the horror film was much better than the first movie.

6. The train robbers took all of the passengers' money, then _____ the conductor and rode off on their horses.

7. When his _____ was stolen, Carl was forced to walk to work.

8. As the ground around the well dries up, the opening of the well will _____ until it disappears.

Fill in the blank with the best word from the choices below. One word will not be used.

convection   distracted   abducted   prosecuted

9. A sign in the shop window warned that shoplifters would be _____ to the full extent of the law.

10. _____ in the hot spring brought warmer currents of water to the surface.

11. Both music and loud noises _____ Isaiah when he was trying to work.

Exercise III. Choose the set of words that best completes the sentence.

1. The idea of a(n) _____ to the novel was _____ to many people who had enjoyed the author's other books.
   A. convection; abducting
   B. sequence; distracting
   C. vehicle; attractive
   D. sequel; attractive

2. A(n) _____ of events, including a drought and construction projects, led the mouth of the river to _____ to a quarter of its original size.
   A. sequel; abduct
   B. vehicle; produce
   C. sequence; contract
   D. conduct; distract

3. After the way the Senator _____ the investigation, I will not be surprised if the District Attorney decides to _____ her.
   A. conducted; prosecute
   B. contracted; abduct
   C. abducted; produce
   D. prosecuted; produce

4.   While Fred made lots of noise to _____ the policeman, John _____ the rare bird and
      drove off with it.
      A. contract; prosecuted
      B. distract; abducted
      C. abduct; produce
      D. abduct; distract

5.   The force of _____ in the pot of water _____ a layer of heat at the surface.
      A. sequence; conducted
      B. sequel; produced
      C. vehicle; abducted
      D. convection; produced

Exercise IV. Complete the sentence by inferring information about the italicized word from its context.

1.   If the customer hadn't *distracted* Juan, the change she received would have...

2.   Dr. Ellis said that even though all the test answers were right, the *sequence* was wrong, so...

3.   Because Tanisha *conducted* the club meeting so well, she...

**Exercise V. Fill in the blank with the word from the Unit that best completes the sentence, using the root
we supply as a clue. Then, answer the questions that follow the paragraphs.**

The Korean War, a conflict between the Communists in the North and the anti-Communists in the South, lasted from June 25, 1950, to July 27, 1953, and is commonly known as the "forgotten" war. After World War II, the country was tired of fighting. To make the new war more _____ (TRACT), President Harry Truman referred to it as a "police effort." Many people were unaware an actual war was being fought until troops returned from Asia.

The Korean War began because of the forced division of Korea after World War II. Prior to 1945, Japan occupied Korea, but by the end of World War II, the Soviet Union had taken control of the northern part. The United States began to fear the Soviet Union would eventually control all of Korea, so the U.S. took control of the southern half up to the 38th parallel. Both of the divisions in Korea appointed leaders, and regimes emerged. The Koreans in the south elected Syngman Rhee, a known anti-Communist, who had lived in the United States for decades. The activity in the northern regime was _____(DUCT) by Kim Il Sung, a known Communist guerrilla.

Upon taking power, Kim immediately redistributed land so that a few wealthy Koreans would own most of it, which forced many Koreans to live as impoverished tenant farmers. Some Koreans in the South agreed with Kim's actions and rebelled against Rhee, their own leader, but the United States and United Nations backed Rhee, who wanted to stop communism from taking over in the South as it had the North. Their combined efforts appeared to defeat the guerrillas, so the United States demilitarized South Korea and gave light weapons to the remaining militia.

In an international press conference on January 5, 1950, Secretary of State Dean Acheson publicly vowed to defend Japan, the Ryukyu Islands, and the Philippine Islands from Communists, but he left out Korea. The North Koreans, who had many tanks and armored vehicles, heard of this vow and knew that without the support of the United States and its allies, they could take control of South Korea by force. When the United States realized the anti-Communists in the South were no longer resisting communism, U.S. forces entered the war under the leadership of General Douglas MacArthur. The United States got United Nations' approval and a mandate for action. Eventually, the United States, United Nations, and others supported South Korea; and the Communist countries of the Soviet Union and China became involved in the campaign in support of North Korea.

After three years of fighting, the North Koreans claimed victory. The war ended with a cease-fire agreement, a demilitarized zone at the 38th parallel, but there was never a peace treaty. This war will never be forgotten because it gave the United States a part in the Cold War. Thankfully, the Cold War ended, but the world still struggles with other obstacles to peace and probably always will. The Korean War and its history, therefore, continue to influence the world today.

1. What, according to the article, was the main cause of the Korean War?
    A. division of land
    B. religion
    C. the Soviet Union
    D. the United Nations

2. What was the political system of the ruler in the North?
    A. Catholicism
    B. guerrilla warfare
    C. Communism
    D. Democracy

3. Why did the United States enter the war?
    A. to fight the spread of Communism
    B. to protect Kim Il Sung
    C. to help the United Nations
    D. to train the army

4. Why is the Korean War called the "forgotten war"?
    A. It is not studied in the history books.
    B. Many citizens did not know it was an actual war.
    C. The Koreans tried to cover up the fighting.
    D. Few troops died.

Exercise VI. Drawing on your knowledge of roots and words in context, read the following selection and define the *italicized* words. If you cannot figure out the meaning of the words on your own, look them up in a dictionary. Note that *sub* means "under, following," and *de* means "from."

The heavy rainfall that we experienced here in Pondtown and the *subsequent* floods that put our streets under water resulted in the closing of schools, banks, and city offices for many weeks. Even if you had heard nothing about the rain and floods, you could *deduce* that something very bad had happened. Power lines were down, cars were stranded in the road, and not a single person could be seen outside.

UNIT SIXTEEN

GRAV
Latin GRAVIS, "heavy"

GRAVE (grāv) *adj.* Very serious
The city was running out of water quickly, and the situation would soon become *grave*.
syn: grim   ant: lighthearted

GRAVITY (grav´ə tē) *n.* Seriousness
Brett's little brother didn't understand the *gravity* of their father's losing his job.
         ant: insignificance

The GRAVITY of the announcement really PULLED DOWN the mood in the room.

You have probably heard gravity *used to mean "the force that holds people and things on the Earth." How do you think this definition is related to* gravity, *meaning "seriousness"?*

LEV, LEVER
Latin LEVIS, "light"
LEVARE, LEVATUM, "to lift up"

LEVITATE (lev´ə tāt) *v.* To cause to hover or float above the ground
For a moment, the ball appeared to *levitate* above the basket.

ALLEVIATE (ə lē´ vē āt) *v.* To make better or less serious
L. ad, "towards," + levis = *lighten the burden towards*
The doctor told Jackie she could *alleviated* her back pain by improving her posture.
syn: lighten   ant: worsen

ELEVATE (el´ə vāt) *v.* To lift up
L. e, "out of," + levare = *to lift out of*
The emergency room staff decided to *elevate* Darren's leg to slow the flow of blood.

LEVERAGE (lev´ er əj) *n.* Something which gives help or advantage
Three strong men couldn't move the car, so they used a fallen tree limb for *leverage*.
syn: effectiveness   ant: disadvantage

BRUT
Latin BRUTUS, "heavy"

BRUTALITY (brōō tal´ ə tē)   *n.*   Cruel violence
The dictator showed his *brutality* when he had three disloyal generals executed in public.
syn: savagery   *ant*: kindness

BRUTE (brōōt)   *adj.*   Not showing reason; animal-like; raw
Using the *brute* power in their trunks and tusks, elephants can easily tear up entire trees.

ant: humane

PRESS
Latin PRIMERE, PRESSUM, "press"

OPPRESS (ə pres´)   *v.*   To keep down by force
L. ob, "against," + pressum = *press against*
Throughout history, weak societies have been *oppressed* by stronger ones.
syn: persecute   *ant*: liberate

IMPRESS (im pres´)   *v.*   1. To have a strong effect on
                                2. Make a mark with; strongly convey
L. in, "in," + pressum = *press into*
1. Gloria's knowledge of sports trivia *impressed* the host of the show.
2. My mother *impressed* upon me the importance of being honest.
syn: affect; influence

Ⅲ *You can impress the mark of your shoe into the mud; you can also impress an idea upon someone's mind. Either way, you leave some trace of your presence behind.*

EXERCISES - UNIT SIXTEEN

Exercise I. Complete the sentence in a way that shows you understand the meaning of the italicized vocabulary word.

1.   The dream *impressed* itself strongly upon my mind because…

2.   Ty often got what he wanted through *brute* strength rather than…

3.   The *gravity* of the town's economic situation became clear when…

4.   The feather seemed to *levitate* in midair rather than…

5.   Because the king had *oppressed* his subjects for years, they…

6.   My instructor *elevated* the piano bench so that…

7.   In order to gain some *leverage* during her job interview, Larissa…

8.   The *brutality* of the crime described in the newspaper made many readers…

9.   To *alleviate* some of this stress headaches, John decided to…

10. When we saw the doctor's *grave* expression, we wondered if…

Exercise II. Fill in the blank with the best word from the choices below. One word will not be used.

   oppress   brute   grave   levitated   elevate

1.   After a series of massive tornadoes, many of the farms were in _____ condition.

2.   The movers had to _____ the piano to window level because it would not fit through the door.

3.   Laura was so bossy that she often tried to _____ her other family members.

4.   The ghost did not walk along the ground like a human being, but _____ a few inches above the ground.

Fill in the blank with the best word from the choices below. One word will not be used.

brute   alleviate   leverage   impress

5.   Taking a walk in the park always helps to _____ my sadness.

6.   The _____ force of the wrestler brought his opponent to the floor.

7.   The United Nations needed to _____ upon its members the necessity of sending troops to separate warring countries.

Fill in the blank with the best word from the choices below. One word will not be used.

gravity   brutality   leverage   grave

8.   No one could believe that the hunter had used such _____ to take down his prey.

9.   The fact that Corey had been innocently crossing the street when he was hit by the car gave him some _____ in the court case.

10.   Even though he was aware of the _____ required of him at the funeral, Len could not resist making a few jokes.

Exercise III. Choose the set of words that best completes the sentence.

1.   The patient's condition is quite _____, but doctors can _____ some of his pain with medication.
       A. grave; alleviate
       B. brute; levitate
       C. brute; impress
       D. grave; oppress

2.   One student tried to use his position as a Teacher's Assistant as _____ to _____ his classmates, but they laughed at his attempts.
       A. elevated; levitate
       B. levitate; oppress
       C. leverage; impress
       D. alleviate; oppress

3.   The principal tried to _____ the seriousness of the meeting to keep everyone aware of the _____ and danger of the situation.
       A. levitate; leverage
       B. elevate; gravity
       C. oppress; brutality
       D. grave; leverage

4. The construction workers wished they could _____ the heavy box in some way, but they had to use _____ strength and a lot of energy.
   A. oppress; grave
   B. alleviate; brute
   C. elevate; grave
   D. levitate; brute

5. The _____ of the king's nature was clear from the way he _____ any people who disagreed with him.
   A. elevation; levitated
   B. brutality; leverage
   C. gravity; impressed
   D. brutality; oppressed

Exercise IV. Complete the sentence by inferring information about the italicized word from its context.

1. If Charlie seems *grave* when he boards the bus, his classmates might assume that...

2. Because Constance wanted to *alleviate* the poverty of the beggar, she...

3. If a group of people feels *oppressed* because they cannot practice their religion, they might...

Exercise V. Fill in the blank with the word from the Unit that best completes the sentence, using the root we supply as a clue. Then, answer the questions that follow the paragraphs.

The scene is easy to imagine. The fortune-teller sits in a long, flowing dress with her hair tied back in a bright scarf. She is surrounded by the tools of her trade. In the room, her customers find candles _____ (PRESS) with odd symbols, cards with unusual pictures, and, of course, a large crystal ball. This image of the fortune-teller is a popular one in books and movies, and it may cause some to be very curious about fortune-telling. However, even with all the hype, no one can really predict the future.

People are lured to fortune-tellers because of the promise of learning about what will happen before it actually occurs. They want information about love, work, and family, and they want assistance in making decisions in their personal lives. Some people simply want to be prepared for tomorrow, while others want a guarantee that nothing bad will happen. The fortune-teller seems to _____ (LEV) the worries that many have about their lives. People believe knowing the future today will allow them to better handle their problems and concerns as they appear. In reality though, the fortune-teller cannot truly help those who look for this information.

Even with crystal balls and candles, a fortune-teller cannot know what twists of fate may occur in life. While a fortune-teller may provide a great deal of entertainment, there is no realistic way to faithfully predict the future.

At best, a fortune-teller can learn the wants and fears of a client and make predictions to _____ (LEV) the hopes of one person and confirm the darkest fears of another. Fortune-tellers can hint at terrific treasure and warn of _____ (GRAV) danger, but they can never know for certain what is going to happen until it happens. It is simply impossible to see the future.

The future is different for every single person, and the future changes with every decision the person makes. An individual's future is based on personality, friends and family, interests and hobbies, luck, and many other parts of life. There are just too many factors that make up a person and a future for anyone to predict. Besides the stories in books and movies, there is no reason to believe that pretty props and differently dressed people can reduce the complicated life of a person to a meaningful prediction.

Perhaps one day, scientists may discover a logical way to predict the future events in an individual's life. Until then, those who desire to know what will happen next will have to rely on the glass beads and lucky dates of the traditional figure of the fortune-teller. However, anyone who seeks the advice of such a person must remember the information might make an interesting story, but it certainly is not a barometer for the facts!

1. Why do people go to a fortune-teller, according to the passage?
   A. There is scientific proof for predictions.
   B. They are lonely for someone to talk to.
   C. They want advice for major decisions.
   D. They want to see characters from movies.

2. What does the author believe about fortune telling?
   A. There is no realistic way to predict the future.
   B. There is a factual way to predict the future.
   C. Fortune telling is a smart business.
   D. Fortune-tellers help their customers.

3. Which title would best describe the essay?
   A. The Benefits of Fortune Telling
   B. The Truth of Fortune Telling
   C. Fortune-Tellers In the Movies
   D. Fortune-Tellers Influence Lives

4. In the essay, the author intends to convince readers to believe which idea?
   A. They should consult a fortune-teller before making decisions.
   B. They should consider fortune-tellers entertainment only.
   C. They should never go to fortune-tellers for any reason.
   D. They should believe in fortune-tellers with scientific proof.

Exercise VI. Drawing on your knowledge of roots and words in context, read the following selection and define the *italicized* words. If you cannot figure out the meaning of the words on your own, look them up in a dictionary. Note that *sup*, from *sub*, means "under."

Although the wedding was supposed to be a serious event, the groom could not resist making a joke as he walked towards the altar. In this moment of *levity*, he drew laughter from everyone seated in the church. Even the priest, who was known for his stern temper, and who hardly ever laughed, could not *suppress* a smile when he heard the humorous words of the groom.

UNIT SEVENTEEN

LONG
Latin LONGUS, "long"

ELONGATE   (ē lôn´ gāt)   *v.*   To make longer
L. e, "out of," + longus = *to make something longer out of*
The amoeba *elongated* itself so it could get through the tiny opening.
syn: stretch   *ant:* condense; shorten

PROLONG   (prō lông´)   *v.*   To extend the time of; draw out
L. pro, "forward," + longus = *to push forward longer*
Each minute that Leonard had to wait for the package *prolonged* his nervousness.
syn: draw out   *ant:* abbreviate

BREV
Latin BREVIS, "brief"

ABBREVIATE   (ə brē´ vē āt)   *v.* To make shorter
L. ad, "towards," + brevis = *towards the short*
The owner of the company *abbreviated* the meeting to catch a plane that was supposed to leave in ten minutes.
syn: shorten   *ant:* prolong

BREVITY   (bre´ vi tē)   *n.*   Shortness
In the book on making a speech, Keith read that *brevity* is more important than covering every fact about a subject.

DENS
Latin   DENSUS, "thick"

DENSITY   (den´ sə tē)   *n.*   Thickness
Jamaal performed an experiment that proved that two blocks of wood of different sizes had the same *density*.
syn: solidity

CONDENSE   (kən dens´)   *v.*   To make thicker or shorter
L. con, "completely," + densus = *completely thicken*
The cement wasn't ready to be used until it *condensed* a little more.
syn: contract   *ant:* expand

III *The density of something is more than its weight. Density refers to how solid it is, how tightly its parts (atoms) fit together. That is why two objects that weigh the same might easily be different sizes: their density is different.*

MAC, MEAG
Latin MACER, "thin"

EMACIATED   (ə mā´ shē āt əd)   *adj.*   Very thin; starving
L. e, "very," + macer = *made very thin*
syn: scrawny   *ant*: plump

MEAGER   (mē´ ger)   *adj.*   Not plentiful
Patricia's parents think that her weight is too low because she picks at her food
and eats only a *meager* amount.
syn: slight   *ant*: abundant

The hunter returned from his trip with only
one MEAGER BEAVER.

TEND, TENT
Latin TENDERE, TENTUS, "to stretch"

ATTENTIVE   (ə ten´ tiv)   *adj.*   Interested and careful
L. ad, "towards," + tendere = *stretching toward*
No matter how sleepy my dog seems, if you have a biscuit for him, he's immediately *attentive* and alert.
syn: studious   *ant*: distracted

INTEND   (in tend´)   *v.*   To mean; to have in one's mind
L. in, "at," + tendere = *to stretch at*
What do you think Hector *intended* by that comment about the substitute teacher?
syn: plan

Ⅲ *How did the Latin*
macer *become the*
English meager? *When*
macer *entered French, its*
"c" became a "g." From
there, it was just a short
jump to the English
meager.

EXERCISES - UNIT SEVENTEEN

Exercise I. Complete the sentence in a way that shows you understand the meaning of the italicized vocabulary word.

1.   Andrea felt that the fire at school had been *intended* to…

2.   Although our supply of food for the trip was *meager*, we…

3.   The builder decided to *elongate* the kitchen in the house so that…

4.   The *brevity* of the candidate's speech made us wonder if…

5.   The television program about World War II had to *condense* its story because…

6.   The newspaper had to *abbreviate* the President's name because…

7.   When we saw the *emaciated* victims of the war, we knew they had…

8.   The *density* of the snow may change our skiing plans because…

9.   Kody was told to be more *attentive* in class, so he…

10.   Mark didn't want to *prolong* his sick cat's suffering, so he…

Exercise II. Fill in the blank with the best word from the choices below. One word will not be used.

    attentive   prolong   elongated   abbreviated   emaciated

1.   We were amazed that the kitten who had once been _____ and starving had grown so plump and healthy.

2.   Because Darice was such a(n) _____ listener, she never had to ask me to repeat anything.

3.   We found it strange that Angelina _____ her name when writing in French, but wrote it out fully in English.

4.   Rather than _____ the painful medical treatment, the patient plans to seek a new doctor.

Fill in the blank with the best word from the choices below. One word will not be used.

      intended   condense   elongated   brevity

5.   Lionel had to find a way to _____ the materials in the box so that he could fit more into it.

6.   Vince expected a long apology from Rita, so the _____ of her speech surprised him.

7.   The spaghetti maker took short, thick rolls of pasta and _____ them until they were about five inches from end to end.

Fill in the blank with the best word from the choices below. One word will not be used.

      density   emaciated   meager   intended

8.   The _____ amount of rain we got during the month of July was not enough for our crop of corn.

9.   Lead has a higher _____ and weighs more than most other metals.

10.   Because Joe's rude comment was not really _____ to hurt her, Merle decided to forgive him.

Exercise III. Choose the set of words that best completes the sentence.

1.   The baker could not decide whether to _____ the loaf of bread so that it would look larger or _____ it so that the ingredients would taste stronger.
     A. elongate; condense
     B. intend; prolong
     C. prolong; abbreviate
     D. abbreviate; condense

2.   If Walter _____ his diet for many more days, he will start to look _____ and unhealthy.
     A. condenses; attentive
     B. condenses; meager
     C. abbreviates; attentive
     D. prolongs; emaciated

3.   Even though her audience was very _____ and interested, Valerie decided to _____ her speech and leave early.
     A. attentive; abbreviate
     B. meager; emaciate
     C. emaciated; condense
     D. meager; prolong

4.   Was the _____ of the concert _____, or did the band accidentally stop too early?
      A. density; attentive
      B. brevity; intended
      C. elongation; meager
      D. abbreviation; emaciated

5.   The _____ of the soil was very difficult to deal with because there was only a(n) _____
      supply of water to the area.
      A. brevity; prolonged
      B. density; elongated
      C. brevity; intended
      D. density; meager

Exercise IV. Complete the sentence by inferring information about the italicized word from its context.

1.   To *prolong* the suspense of the ghost story, Tamara's dad might…

2.   Because Marina saw pictures of *emaciated* children in Africa, she will probably make the decision to…

3.   Since William tried to *condense* his essay into one page, we could conclude that…

Exercise V. Fill in the blank with the word from the Unit that best completes the sentence, using the root we supply as a clue. Then, answer the questions that follow the paragraphs.

Today, with automobiles, trains and airplanes, it's difficult to comprehend the much slower pace of travel common to American pioneers heading west. Wagon-masters in charge of leading settlers across the plains and Rocky Mountains were happy if they traveled twenty miles in a day. Modern travelers cannot even pretend to understand how people and supplies were moved over vast distances only by animal power. Yet the pioneers endured it because they knew of no other way.

Modern tourists can now get a sense of what it was like to travel by wagon train by visiting two historic sites in southeastern Wyoming: Oregon Trail Ruts and Register Cliff.

The Oregon Trail was the most popular route west; it was almost 2,000 miles, starting at Independence, Missouri and ending in Oregon City, Oregon. This "road" was a dirt path across the plains and through the mountains that was crossed by thousands of emigrants who had made the decision to seek a new life. For over a generation, such a multitude of iron-rimmed wheels rolled across the same stretch of land that a permanent reminder of their presence was carved into the soft sandstone along the bank of the North Platte

River near Guernsey, Wyoming. The Oregon Trail Ruts are a pair of parallel ditches cut into the earth about four feet apart, and, in some places, five feet. A modern traveler can stand in these ruts and attempt to visualize the tremendous migration that not only formed them, but also helped to extend the United States to the Pacific Ocean.

A few miles away is Register Cliff, a sandstone hill where pioneers took a stop in order to carve their names and dates into the mountain wall, announcing to all that they had survived to this point in their journey. _____ (BREV) was important because the wagon masters didn't _____ (TEND) to stay long at any one location, so most of the signatures are initials for first and middle names, with the last name spelled out, followed by the year, but not an exact date.

Most wagon trains reached southeastern Wyoming in July; they had been on the trail since April, and they still had another two months to go, so any delay ran the risk of _____ (LONG) their stay in the Sierra Mountains.

It took six months to travel the Oregon Trail by wagon. Today, tourists can fly from Missouri to Oregon in three hours.

1.   Why did the pioneers carve their names into Register Cliff, according to the article?
     A. vandalism
     B. to mark their progress
     C. fame
     D. It was something they wanted to do.

2.   What was the Oregon Trail?
     A. a paved road to the Pacific Ocean
     B. a dirt trail through to the Sierra Mountains
     C. a dirt trail from the Atlantic to the Pacific Ocean
     D. a 2,000 mile long route

3.   Why did a wagon-master need to reach Wyoming by July?
     A. to avoid the hot weather in the plains
     B. to shorten the time spent in the Sierra Mountains
     C. to find good hunting
     D. to avoid Indians

4.   What is the approximate time it took to cross the Oregon Trail?
     A. two months
     B. the article does not say
     C. one year
     D. six months

Exercise VI. Drawing on your knowledge of roots and words in context, read the following selection and define the *italicized* words. If you cannot figure out the meaning of the words on your own, look them up in a dictionary. Note that *dis* means "apart" and *–evity* means "age, period of life."

Hunger is a problem for the world's adults, but it is especially serious for children. In the United States alone, children in over two million households go hungry. Some of the signs of hunger include sunken cheeks, a change in hair color, and, especially, a *distended* stomach. This bloated and stretched-out belly is a sign that a child is in serious danger. In any country with a serious hunger problem, *longevity* rates are very low; underfed people rarely live past the age of sixty.

UNIT EIGHTEEN

AER, AIR
Latin AER, AERIS, "air"

AERATE (âr´ āt) *v.* To fill with air; to expose to air
Making homemade ice cream is easier if you first *aerate* the cream before adding the flavoring.

AERIAL (âr´ ē əl) *adj.* Done from or in the air
Michelle performed a few *aerial* stunts during the show that proved she could pilot the plane with great skill.

AIRY (âr´ ē) *adj.* Light; not heavy or serious
The pancakes were so *airy* and fluffy that they seemed to melt in Lisa's mouth.

FLAT
Latin FLARE, FLATUM, "to blow"

INFLATE (in flāt´) *v.* To make bigger
Mr. Marbury was sentenced to a year in jail because he illegally *inflated* the price of his company's stock.
syn: pump up

DEFLATE (di flāt´) *v.* To make smaller, make less
To make the hot-air balloon fly lower to the ground, Debbie *deflated* it by releasing some of its air.
syn: puncture

III *To inflate means "to fill with air," but also "to make something seem larger without really increasing its size or value." When the economy is in a period of inflation, for instance, there seems to be a lot of money, but each dollar actually is not worth very much.*

III *Deflate, like inflate, can have two meanings: it can mean "take the air out of," as you would a tire or a beach ball; it can also mean "bring down, make less." If you deflate a child's hopes of getting a pony, the child will probably be very disappointed.*

VENT
Latin VENTILARE, VENTILATUM, "to fan, to blow"

VENTILATE (ven´ ti lāt) *v.* To push air through
The FBI had to *ventilate* the room over and over to remove the poison safely.

HYPERVENTILATE (hī´ pər ven ti lāt) *v.* To breathe too fast
Sally was so afraid of flying that she had to take medicine or she would *hyperventilate* throughout the whole flight.

SPIR
Latin SPIRARE, SPIRATUM, "to breathe"

ASPIRE (a spīr´) *v.* To aim; to have as a goal
L. ad, "towards," + spirare = *to breathe towards*
All his life, Arnold *aspired* to earn a million dollars, but he was unhappy when he finally did.
syn: strive

SPIRITED (spir´ ə təd) *adj.* Having much energy; lively
Bev was a *spirited* young child, and she grew into a lively and friendly adult.
syn: animated   *ant*: dull

EXPIRE (ek spīr´) *v.* To come to an end
L. ex, "out," + spirare = *to breathe out*
Dean didn't pay his yearly fee, so the lease to the storage shed he used *expired*.
syn: run out   *ant*: continue

The EX-FLYER EXPIRED in a plane crash.

▥ *To expire literally means "to breathe out," or "to breathe one's last." Expire is now used to describe anything, not just a life, that comes to an end. A coupon or a carton of milk may expire, just as a person who is very ill may expire.*

EXERCISES - UNIT EIGHTEEN

Exercise I. Complete the sentence in a way that shows you understand the meaning of the italicized vocabulary word.

1. If you don't *aerate* the fish in the tank,...

2. The musical piece sounded light and *airy* to us because...

3. The sales manager decided to *inflate* the cost of shoes in her store so that...

4. The spy took an *aerial* photograph so that...

5. It is important that the greenhouse be properly *ventilated* so that...

6. Roger was afraid he would *hyperventilate* when he met his favorite singer, so he...

7. When Sarah's credit card *expires*, she will have to...

8. Henrietta *aspires* to be a surgeon, so she is studying...

9. Because the horse was so *spirited*, it was difficult to...

10. Esther's performance at the swim meet seemed to *deflate* her pride, but...

Exercise II. Fill in the blank with the best word from the choices below. One word will not be used.

expired   aspire   aerial   airy   ventilated

1.   If you _____ to join the Olympic swimming team, you will need to practice every day.

2.   The designer decided to replace the heavy wool drapes with _____ curtains that seemed to float in the wind.

3.   Christopher noticed that the time allowed for finishing the test had _____, so he put down his pencil.

4.   Damon _____ the stuffy apartment when he opened all the doors and windows.

Fill in the blank with the best word from the choices below. One word will not be used.

    hyperventilated   ventilated   deflated   aerated

5.   When Steve started talking about who was going to be fired, he _____ the happy mood at the office party.

6.   When the accident victim saw his own blood on the ground, he became frightened and _____ until the police told him he would be fine.

7.   The lawn company _____ the soil before fertilizing it.

Fill in the blank with the best word from the choices below. One word will not be used.

    spirited   inflated   aerial   aspired

8.   Tammy enjoyed flying her own plane because she got a great _____ view of the lovely French countryside.

9.   The group of carolers at the door sang a(n) _____ version of the song "Jingle Bells."

10.   Corinne _____ the raft by using an air pump.

Exercise III. Choose the set of words that best completes the sentence.

1.   Unlike the composer's earlier works, which were slow and heavy, this one was both _____ and _____.
     A. inflated; ventilated
     B. aerial; deflated
     C. spirited; airy
     D. spirited; expired

2.   The _____ photo of the dried field showed that the dirt needed to be _____ .
     A. aerial; aerated
     B. spirited; ventilated
     C. hyperventilating; expired
     D. aerial; spirited

3.   The coach's words have _____ Bethany's pride so much that she now _____ to win the gold medal.
     A. aerated; inflates
     B. deflated; expires
     C. inflated; aspires
     D. aspired; ventilates

4.   Unfortunately, it was impossible for the surgeon to _____ one side of the heart without _____ the vein on the other side.
    A.   aerate; aspiring
    B.   ventilate; deflating
    C.   deflate; hyperventilating
    D.   deflate; aspiring

5.   When the paramedics saw their patient wake up and began to _____, they knew she would not_____ in the ambulance.
    A.   deflate; aspire
    B.   hyperventilate; expire
    C.   inflate; aerate
    D.   aspire; ventilate

Exercise IV. Complete the sentence by inferring information about the italicized word from its context.

1. Because Jay's spirits were *deflated* by the story of the man in a wheelchair, he probably…

2. If there's an *aerial* act in the circus, everyone in the audience probably…

3. Becky *aspires* to be a gymnast, so it is possible that she…

Exercise V. Fill in the blank with the word from the Unit that best completes the sentence, using the root we supply as a clue. Then, answer the questions that follow the paragraphs.

More and more, we hear of people affected with asthma, in particular, exercised-induced asthma. Respirators, or inhalers, are now a common sight on school playing fields; in fact, more than seventeen million people, including nearly five million children in the United States suffer from asthma. What exactly is it? How can exercise cause it? Does this mean that people with asthma can never become physically fit?

Asthma is a chronic disease, which means it continues for a long time or it recurs frequently. The basic problem is that air flow in and out of the lungs becomes blocked, making breathing very difficult. Most attacks are brought on by triggers, or factors in the environment, which do not affect non-asthmatics. For example, while a person who does not have asthma would not be affected, an asthmatic might be unusually sensitive to dust mites, air pollutants, or high pollen counts, all of which can cause a bad reaction in the person's bronchial tubes. In exercise-induced asthma, the airways are overly sensitive to sudden changes in temperature and humidity. Under normal circumstances, people breathe through their noses, which makes the air that goes into their lungs warm and humid. However, during strenuous exercise, people tend to breathe through their mouths, allowing colder, drier air to reach the lower passages. When this happens, the asthmatic suffers from wheezing, chest tightness, or shortness of breath.

What actually happens in the body is this: the bronchial tubes react to certain triggers, the muscles around the airways tighten, and this makes air passages narrower. In addition, the lining of the airways becomes swollen and congested with mucus, which further plugs them. Asthmatics may be able to get enough air into their lungs despite the narrowing of the tubes, but it is especially difficult to exhale because the air gets trapped behind the narrow passages. When we breathe in, we _____ (FLAT) our lungs. Asthmatics, however, are unable to _____ (FLAT) their lungs completely because of the narrowed tubes, allowing stale air to stay inside and preventing the exchange of fresh air and oxygen. If the lungs do not get enough oxygen, carbon dioxide can build up in the body, putting the respiratory system under severe stress and placing the person's life in danger. This is why it is important that asthmatics use inhalers, which allow them to inhale medication that will widen the bronchial tubes and improve airflow.

Despite the difficulties that asthma can cause, many people have learned to understand their conditions and become physically fit. For some it means picking sports that allow them, literally, to catch their breaths, such as baseball, wrestling, gymnastics, golf, and short-term track and field events. Those sports, unlike soccer, basketball, field hockey, or long-distance running, do not require continuous activity. Still, other asthmatics have found ways, with proper training and medical treatment, to excel as long-distance runners and basketball players. Many have become Olympians. With help, asthma does not have to keep a person from doing what he or she would like to do.

1. Bronchial tubes can be narrowed by
   A. dust mites.
   B. air pollution.
   C. cold air.
   D. All of the above

2. During strenuous exercise, asthmatics tend to
   A. breathe through their noses.
   B. breathe through their mouths.
   C. be sensitive to warm air.
   D. All of the above.

3. The lung deflates when a person exhales
   A. stale air.
   B. carbon monoxide.
   C. air that he or she has inhaled.
   D. None of the above.

4. This essay is mainly about
   A. how to control asthma.
   B. how athletes deal with asthma.
   C. what happens to the body during an asthma attack.
   D. how people do what they want to do in spite of asthma.

Exercise VI. Drawing on your knowledge of roots and words in context, read the following selection and define the *italicized* words. If you cannot figure out the meaning of the words on your own, look them up in a dictionary. Note that *con* means "together."

The trial of a local doctor charged with *conspiring* to murder a patient went on for more than three weeks. The other suspect in the secret murder plot fled the country, and lawyers on both sides kept presenting new evidence and asking for more time from the judge. When the time finally came for the jury to make its decision, the judge warned the jurors not to *conflate* the facts with their opinions or prejudices. If they mixed up opinion and truth, he said, they would be breaking the sacred trust of the court.

UNIT NINETEEN

NARRAT
NARRARE, NARRATUM, "to tell"

NARRATIVE (naˊ rə tiv) *n.* A story
Just at the most exciting part of the story, Gramps stopped, but he told us that he'd pick up the *narrative* the next night.

NARRATE (naˊ rāt) *v.* To tell a story
The children's librarian was often called upon to *narrate* fairly tales to the Saturday class.
syn: relate

NOUNC
Latin NUNTIARE, NUNTIATUM, "to announce, report, say, speak"

PRONOUNCE (prə nountsˊ) *v.* To speak in a certain way; say aloud
L. pro, "forth," + nuntiare = *to say forth*
Jenna had to look in the dictionary to figure out how to *pronounce* the word.

DENOUNCE (di nountsˊ) *v.* To criticize; to blame
L. de, "down," + nuntiare = *to bring down by speaking*
The angry lawyer publicly *denounced* the judge.
syn: condemn   *ant:* praise

FABUL, FABL
Latin FABULA, "story, fable"

FABULOUS (fabˊ yə ləs) *adj.* Amazing; fantastic
Diana had such a *fabulous* time at Al's party that she decided to help him clean up.
                    ant: bad; poor

FABLED (fāˊ bəld) *adj.* Legendary; famous
Valerie's *fabled* intelligence was the subject of many conversations at school.

III Fabulous *literally means "existing in fables or stories." Today, it means so wonderful or amazing that it seems unreal. The word has been used so often, though, that it has lost some of its power.*

MYTH
Greek MYTHOS, "story"

MYTHICAL   (mith´ i kəl)   *adj.*   Not existing in reality; made up
Even in modern times, many people believe in the *mythical* island called Atlantis.

MYTHOLOGY   (mith ol´ ə jē)   *n.*   Group of stories associated with a subject or
      culture
Ty's favorite subject was Greek *mythology* because he enjoyed stories of gods,
monsters, and heroes.

COUNT
Latin COMPUTARE, "to calculate, reckon, add up"

RECOUNT   (rə kount´)   *v.*   To tell; to describe
L. re, "again," + computare = *to add up again, retell*
Every Christmas, Dad would *recount* the story of how his grandfather escaped
from a prisoner of war camp during World War II.
syn: retell

DISCOUNT   (dis´ kount)   *v.*   To put down; To say or believe something is not
      worth much
L. dis, "away," + computare = *to count away, count as nothing*
Maureen *discounts* Sam's opinion because he has been wrong almost every time in
the past.
syn: dismiss   *ant*: value

*We all DISCOUNT THIS COUNT Dracula because
he's not scary enough.*

*Earlier in this book,
you encountered the
Latin word "putare,"
meaning "think, deter-
mine." Computare
comes from* putare, *but
means "to add up."
When* computare *went
through French, it
became the verb* conter,
*which means both "to
add up (numbers)" and
"to measure out (the
parts of a story)." From
this French word, we get
both* discount *and*
recount.

EXERCISES - UNIT NINETEEN

Exercise I. Complete the sentence in a way that shows you understand the meaning of the italicized vocabulary word.

1.   The sailor's *narrative* of life on the high seas made everyone…

2.   The story of the giant was part of the country's *mythology*, rather than…

3.   The famous mountain-climber will *recount* some of her experiences with…

4.   Jessica *denounced* the actions of the local police because…

5.   Although many ballet dancers *discounted* the talents of the young star, she…

6.   Without the guide to *narrate* our tour, we would have been unable to…

7.   The *fabled* courage of the great warrior…

8.   While we were kept inside by the snow, my brother told *fabulous* tales about…

9.   When Dorothy learned that unicorns were *mythical* creatures, she felt…

10.   Donald found many of the words in the story difficult to *pronounce* because…

Exercise II. Fill in the blank with the best word from the choices below. One word will not be used.

> mythology   narrative   discount   narrates

1.   The messenger was interrupted in the middle of his _____ about what had happened during the battle.

2.   Do not _____ the threat of the volcano, or you may find yourself in great danger.

3.   Mr. Jasper's voice is familiar because he often _____ local television programs.

Fill in the blank with the best word from the choices below. One word will not be used.

pronounce   fabulous   denounce   mythology

4.   Art dreamed up a(n) _____ picture of pink dragons and floating castles.

5.   The principal was afraid he would make a mistake when he tried to _____ the new student's name.

6.   Josh studied Greek and Roman _____ for such a long time that he began to imagine that he had amazing strength like Hercules.

Fill in the blank with the best word from the choices below. One word will not be used.

recount   mythical   fabled   denounced   pronounce

7.   Lady Anne's _____ beauty brought knights from near and far to ask for her hand in marriage.

8.   It was surprising when Evan _____ his teacher, since he had always seemed to like her.

9.   Trisha wondered whether the film she saw was based on a true story or a(n) _____ tale.

10. Rebekah asked Molly to _____ the whole story of the dance to her.

Exercise III. Choose the set of words that best completes the sentence.

1.   Derek's _____ about a(n) _____ car that could fly into outer space won the school's prize for fiction.
     A.   narrative; fabulous
     B.   mythology; narrative
     C.   discounting; pronounced
     D.   recounting; narrating

2.   Nick found it difficult to _____ the radio program because he could not _____ many of the words.
     A.   recount; discount
     B.   discount; pronounce
     C.   narrate; pronounce
     D.   discount; narrate

3.   Experts tend to _____ the stories about the giant, saying they are _____ rather than true.
     A.   discount; mythical
     B.   recount; narrative
     C.   denounce; pronounced
     D.   narrate; fabled

4.   Even if Jane _____ the story exactly as she remembers it, Georgina will probably _____ her for lying.
      A.   pronounces; recount
      B.   recounts; denounce
      C.   recounts; narrate
      D.   discounts; narrate

5.   Much of the country's _____ centers on the amazing deeds of a(n) _____ hero who was ten feet tall.
      A.   recounting; mythical
      B.   discounting; narrative
      C.   narrative; mythology
      D.   mythology; fabled

Exercise IV. Complete the sentence by inferring information about the italicized word from its context.

1.   When one wrestler *denounces* the other, the crowd may…

2.   If the police were angry that no one could *recount* the robbery details, it might mean that…

3.   If Angelique forgets a part and cannot finish her *narrative* of her trip to Washington, it may be because…

Exercise V. Fill in the blank with the word from the Unit that best completes the sentence, using the root we supply as a clue. Then, answer the questions that follow the paragraphs.

Samuel Langhorne Clemens was born in 1835 in a small town in Missouri. He was the fourth and youngest child of John Clemens, a businessman and legal official, and his wife Jane.

John Clemens was plagued by financial troubles, and the family was often in debt. When Samuel was four, his father moved the family to Hannibal, Missouri, a thriving town on the Mississippi River, hoping to take advantage of the financial opportunities there. He had little luck. Samuel, however, did benefit from the experience: he got to spend his childhood observing the lively and eccentric inhabitants of the riverside towns. He dreamed of one day piloting a steamboat.

He also became familiar with the realities of the slave trade. Hannibal was a thriving port city, and slaves were bought and sold there As a young boy, Samuel saw a slaveowner beat a slave to death with a piece of iron. Later, another slave ran away and was murdered, and Samuel and his friends found the slave's mutilated corpse. The Clemens family itself owned slaves, but as John Clemens lost money,

he was forced to sell them off. The last slave, Jenny, was sold in 1842.

In 1847, John Clemens, deeply in debt, died. Samuel was forced to take up a trade. His brother Orion had started a newspaper in Hannibal and allowed him to work there as a printer; occasionally, Samuel would also contribute articles or stories. This was the beginning of his life as a writer.

He did not lack exciting experiences to write about. During the 1850s, he found work on a riverboat, as he had hoped. He received his pilot's license in 1859, but the Civil War broke out before he could get much experience. He then briefly formed a military outfit with other young men from Hannibal, but they disbanded after two weeks. Since Orion had been appointed governor of Nevada, Sam decided to go there. The Comstock Lode, a major gold deposit, had been discovered in 1848; Sam caught "gold rush fever" and spent the next few years prospecting.

At the same time, he submitted articles about his experience as a miner to a local newspaper. It was in a(n) _____(NARRAT) written for this publication that he signed the name by which American readers would soon know him. It was taken from a phrase used by river-boat pilots testing the depth of a river: if they could "mark twain," or measure at least two fathoms down, the river was deep enough to travel on.

As Mark Twain, Clemens wrote some of the most famous, funny, and moving passages in American literature, filled with _____(FABUL) detail and sharp insight. His works include *The Adventures of Tom Sawyer, The Adventures of Huckleberry Finn, A Connecticut Yankee in King Arthur's Court,* a nonfiction account of life on the Mississippi River, a satirical novel about the Gilded Age, and numerous essays and short stories. Much of his writing drew on his experiences growing up in Hannibal. He was popular both among American readers and literary critics.

Unfortunately, Twain's later life was not as happy as his childhood. He did not manage money well; to pay off his debts, he was forced to go on a long, exhausting literary tour. Three of his four children, then his wife, died before him. Finally, in April 1910, Twain himself died. Despite the sadness of his final years, he was widely beloved, and he remains one of the most valued and important American writers.

1. Samuel Clemens started working for his brother Orion because
   A. he wanted to be a writer.
   B. he wanted to make new friends in Missouri.
   C. Orion forced him to.
   D. his father had died and left the family in debt.

2. From the passage, *prospecting* means
   A. treating the sick.
   B. looking for gold.
   C. walking around.
   D. waiting for someone.

3. The name that Clemens signed himself by, "Mark Twain," shows
   A. his desire to become a politician.
   B. his frustration at being in debt.
   C. his close ties to the Mississippi River.
   D. his love of his family.

4. Mark Twain's childhood on the Mississippi
   A. influenced his writing.
   B. was the subject of his first newspaper article.
   C. was not as easy as his later years.
   D. was unusual because his family owned slaves.

Exercise VI. Drawing on your knowledge of roots and words in context, read the following selection and define the *italicized* words. If you cannot figure out the meaning of the words on your own, look them up in a dictionary. Not that *ac*, from *ad*, means "toward," and *re* means "back, away."

When asked to give an *account* of his experiences in the war, the soldier told us of terrible suffering and the pain of seeing his best friends die. Although he was proud to have defended his country, he hoped that the world's problems could now be solved in a way that did not involve bloodshed and violence. From this moment on, he said, he would *renounce* war and work for peace in every way possible.

UNIT TWENTY

IDEAL
Latin IDEALIS, "perfect"

IDEALISTIC (ī dēl is´ tik) *adj.* Believing in the idea of perfection or a perfect world
Trent is so *idealistic* that he gives money to any organization supporting animal rights, even if he's never heard of it before.
syn: starry-eyed   *ant*: realistic

IDEAL (ī dēl´) *adj.* Perfectly suitable
At six feet tall, Leo is the *ideal* height for the lead part in the play.
                    ant: imperfect

IDEALIZE (ī dēl´ īz) *v.* To think of as perfect
Marsha *idealized* Scott so much that she was blind to the many faults he had.
                    ant: criticize

SCIEN
Latin SCIRE, SCITUM, "to know"

CONSCIENCE (kon´ shəns) *n.* The part of the mind which tells the difference between right and wrong
Jamie found a wallet, but didn't return it, which made her *conscience* bother her all day long.

SCIENTIFIC (si ən tif´ ik) *adj.* Based on proven facts
Despite the many *scientific* discoveries made in outer space, many people continue to believe that man should never explore beyond Earth.

SAV
Latin SAPERE, "to know"

SAVVY (sa´ vē) *n.* Cleverness; understanding
The mayor's political *savvy* helped him regain the lead and win the election.
syn: know-how

SAVOR (sa´ vər) *v.* To take time to enjoy
We *savored* the stew we had cooked over the fire, knowing we would not eat again before the end of the hike.
syn: linger over   *ant:* rush through

I SAVOR the FLAVOR of ketchup on a banana split.

CERT
Latin CERTARE, CERTATUM, "to decide, determine"
CERTUS, "determined, fixed, certain"

CERTIFY (ser´ tə fī) *v.* To prove good or true; declare correct
The college needed to have its instructors *certify* that their college records were up-to-date.
syn: validate   *ant:* question

CERTAINTY (ser´ ten tē) *n.* Something not in doubt
Out of the entire class, only two students knew the answer to the math problem with any degree of *certainty*.

CONCERTED (kən ser´ təd) *adj.* Done together; combined
The United Nations put together a *concerted* action by fifteen countries to try to combat world hunger.
syn: concentrated   *ant:* scattered

ASCERTAIN (a sûr tān´) *v.* To figure out through reasoning
How will we *ascertain* that the rocket has taken off?

III Why does the Latin sapere *have a "p," while the words we get from it have a "v"? To know the answer, you must know that both* savor *and* savvy *came through French before we English-speakers got them. The French verb meaning "to know," which comes from* sapere, *is* savoir. Savor *and* savvy *are still very close to this French word.*

EXERCISES - UNIT TWENTY

Exercise I. Complete the sentence in a way that shows you understand the meaning of the italicized vocabulary word.

1.   When a special panel of experts was called in to *certify* the lottery results...

2.   We decided that lemon cake would be *ideal* for our picnic because...

3.   Because the methods used in the research project were not *scientific*...

4.   Shondra wanted to *savor* every moment of her birthday party because...

5.   Elka always did what her *conscience* told her to do because...

6.   The basketball fans made a *concerted* effort to yell very loud so...

7.   Danny has enough financial *savvy* that...

8.   Although rain seemed to be a *certainty*, our camping trip...

9.   The painter tended to *idealize* the scenes he painted, rather than...

10.   The volunteers cleaning the polluted beach were all young and *idealistic*, so they...

Exercise II. Fill in the blank with the best word from the choices below. One word will not be used.

idealistic   savvy   ideal   scientific   ascertain

1.   Wilma believes that it is fine to be _____ as long as you don't lose touch with reality.

2.   Lars does not have enough real estate _____ to make financial decisions.

3.   The detective tried to be _____ when investigating the horrible crime, but found that his emotions got in his way.

4.   The researchers were trying to _____ whether the drug was dangerous for children.

Fill in the blank with the best word from the choices below. One word will not be used.

idealizes   conscience   ideal   certainty

5.   My brother accused me of having no _____ when he learned I had stolen money from him.

6.   I believe that Sharice _____ her favorite movie star; she believes he can do no wrong.

7.   Although the tools in the operating room were not _____ for the surgery, they worked well enough.

Fill in the blank with the best word from the choices below. One word will not be used.

scientific   savored   certify   certainty

8.   Barbara _____ the pride she felt the moment she won the cross-country race.

9.   There is no way to _____ the report about the Prime Minister, but we believe it is true.

10.   "The only _____ in my job," said the doctor, "is that people will get sick."

Exercise III. Choose the set of words that best completes the sentence.

1.   JP was a(n) _____ young man who always followed his own _____.
A.   ideal; conscience
B.   scientific; certainty
C.   idealistic; conscience
D.   scientific; savvy

2.   Kit will be a(n) _____ bank manager because he has financial _____ .
A.   scientific; certainty
B.   ideal; savvy
C.   scientific; idealistic
D.   conscience; savvy

3.   I have dreamed about and _____ my vacation for a long time, so I will probably _____ every moment of the trip.
A.   idealized; certify
B.   savored; certify
C.   idealized; savor
D.   savored; ascertain

4. We needed to _____ whether Fergus was telling the truth, so we asked his mother to _____ his story.
    A. idealize; savor
    B. ascertain; certify
    C. certify; savor
    D. ascertain; idealize

5. After a lot of _____ study, the doctors said that a cure for the disease was a(n) _____.
    A. scientific; certainty
    B. savvy; ideal
    C. scientific; conscience
    D. idealistic; conscience

Exercise IV. Complete the sentence by inferring information about the italicized word from its context.

1. If you want to *savor* the taste of your meal, too much salt might…

2. Since Bette and Jay made a *concert*ed effort to elect their favorite candidate, they'll probably be disappointed if…

3. Because Ben has poker *savvy*, he usually…

Exercise V. Fill in the blank with the word from the Unit that best completes the sentence, using the root we supply as a clue. Then, answer the questions that follow the paragraphs.

Sigmund Freud is the best known of several pioneering psychoanalysts of the twentieth century. Born in 1856, Freud lived most of his life in Vienna.

Freud began his career as a physician. He received patients suffering from hysteria, a condition of extreme and uncontrollable anxiety. His interest in the human mind led him to carefully observe and reflect on the suffering of these patients. After intensive study and analysis, Freud came up with his major principles of psychoanalysis. A main part of Freud's psychoanalytic technique employed talking as therapy, called "free association," in which patients say whatever comes to mind. In this way, doctor and patient uncover internal conflicts, which are based in the unconscious mind and which, according to Freud, are created in childhood. The practice of psychiatry still relies on the insights and principles that Freud stated at the turn of the twentieth century.

Freud's approach was _____ (SCIEN). In fact, he is credited with creating the field of psychology, under which the workings of the mind are explained. In other words, there are mental patterns and processes which are common to everyone.

Freud published his most famous book, *The Interpretation of Dreams*, in 1895. In it, Freud _____ (CERT) that dreams are meaningful, and that they are windows to the unconscious. Especially in combination with free association, dreams reveal aspects of the unconscious. Freud divided the unconscious into three parts: the id, the ego, and the superego, which work together, or sometimes against each other, to fulfill human beings' desires. The study of the unconscious is what distinguishes Freud's psychoanalysis from all previous approaches to mental health. In fact, Freud showed that the unconscious played a role in everyone's everyday life.

Freud contributed greatly to society's understanding of childhood development. He outlined the stages through which all children grow and declared that how parents and caretakers manage these stages affects how children grow up. The experience of growing up, then, is impressed on the unconscious and, in turn, is revealed in mental health or mental illness in adulthood.

By the time Freud died in 1939, he had understood the human mind as no other had before or has since.

1.   What is the main idea of the passage?
      A. Freud was a great man.
      B. Freud had an unconscious mind.
      C. Freud analyzed dreams.
      D. Freud studied and developed a theory of how the mind works.

2.   What is the benefit of free association, according to Freud's theory of psychoanalysis?
      A. It reveals the unconscious.
      B. It is fun for patients to talk about anything they want.
      C. Patients feel free to talk openly.
      D. Psychiatrists like to listen.

3.   What are the three components of the unconscious mind?
      A. id, conscious, and ego
      B. ego, superego, and superman
      C. id, ego, and superego
      D. id, superid, and ego

4.   What is the best title for the article?
      A. Sigmund Freud's Contribution to Psychology
      B. Dreams and the Unconscious Mind
      C. Psychoanalysis and the Unconscious
      D. Freud: A Great Man

Exercise VI. Drawing on your knowledge of roots and words in context, read the following selection and define the *italicized* words. If you cannot figure out the meaning of the words on your own, look them up in a dictionary. Note that *omni* means "all."

Professor Harold was a *savant* who had published twenty books and could speak nine languages. He was an expert in law, medicine and literature, but he found time to teach classes at both the local university and high school. His students were so amazed by his knowledge that they began to think of him as *omniscient*. When the Professor heard about this, he laughed and said humbly, "How could I know everything? I barely know anything!"

Book II

abhor
abundant
accelerated
administer
admission
advisable
agile
agitate
allege
amnesty
anarchy
annals
annual
annuity
antediluvian
anticipate
appreciative
arbiter
arbitrary
arbitrate
archaic
arid
aspersions
assiduous
astronomical
autonomous
avail
castigate
cataclysmic
celestial
censor
censure
chastened
chastise
chronic
chronology
cloister
cohabitation
commensurate
composure
conceive
condone
confines
connoisseur
consolidate
conspicuous
contemporaneous
contemporary
corroborate
deceptive
deify
deign
deity
deluge
demented
demote
depreciate
derivative
desist
despicable
deter
detract
diagnosis

differentiate
dilute
dimension
disclose
discourse
disdain
disperse
dissident
donor
durable
duration
editorial
emergent
enact
enduring
enumerate
ergonomic
evident
exaggerated
exceptional
excursion
exhibit
exhume
exponential
extol
extract
finite
formidable
forte
fortitude
founder
frequent
fugitive
fundamental
fusion
horrific
humility
hypothesis
idiom
idiosyncrasy
immense
immerse
immovable
imposition
impunity
inconstant
indeterminate
indignant
infrequent
ingest
innumerable
inoculate
insidious
instantaneous
insular
insulate
inter
intercept
interminable
intersperse
intimidate
intrepid
intuitive
inveterate

invigorate
irreverent
jurisdiction
jurisprudence
litigant
litigation
magisterial
magistrate
matriarch
mentality
minister
mnemonic
mobile
monotheism
nebulous
nemesis
nimbus
nonplussed
nontraditional
notorious
ocular
omission
pantheon
parenthetical
participant
perjure
persistent
plurality
polytheistic
preliminary
preside
prodigal
prognosis
punitive
ration
rational
reactionary
reconnaissance
redundant
reference
refine
refuge
refuse
reinstate
repository
residual
respective
revere
revise
rivulet
robust
sanctify
sanction
sanctuary
sanctum
seclude
sedentary
single
singular
solidarity
sparse
stellar
subliminal
submerge

submissive
subpoena
subsidiary
subsist
subterfuge
subterranean
suggestible
supersede
surgical
surplus
suspect
syndicate
synthesize
tempo
terminal
terrestrial
terrorize
timorous
torrent
torrid
trepidation
tutelage
unrivaled
valiant
valor
veteran
vigorous
vista
volatile

Book III

abjure
abstain
accord
adept
affable
affiliate
affluent
agenda
alias
alienate
allegation
alleviate
alteration
altercation
alternate
amble
ambulatory
amiable
amicable
analogous
animosity
anonymous
antagonist
antagonize
antebellum
antibiotic
antonym
aptitude
aristocracy
assonance
audit
auditory
bellicose

belligerence
benefactor
benevolent
benign
bibliophile
biodegradable
bureaucrat
cadence
casualty
cede
circumspect
cognitive
cognizant
collapse
concession
confound
conjure
consecutive
cordial
corporeal
corpulent
courier
decadent
delegate
denomination
deplete
dialogue
dictum
digress
dilate
diminish
discord
disenchanted
dismal
dispel
disposition
dissemble
dissonance
divest vested
domineering
edict
effigy
elapse
elucidate
enamored
enjoin
enunciate
equanimity
equilibrium
equitable
exacting
execution
expatriate
expedient
figment
filial
formative
genealogy
gradualism
herbivorous
homogenized
homonym
immortalize
impart

impartial
impediment
implement
impose
imprecise
improvise
inalienable
inaudible
incantation
incision
inclusive
incognito
inconclusive
inconsequential
incorporate
incur
indecisive
indicted
indomitable
ineffable
inept
infantile
infuse
inhibit
iniquity
injunction
invidious
invoke
leaven
legacy
legislative
legitimize
levity
lucid
magnanimous
magnate
magnetic
magnify
malevolent
malicious
maternal
matriculate
matron
megalomaniac
megalopolis
mellifluous
metabolism
metamorphosis
metaphorical
microcosm
microscopic
miniscule
minute
misinformation
monlithic
monogamy
monologue
monopolize
morbid
moribund
mortify
nomenclature
nominal
noxious

omnivorous
partisan
paternal
patricide
patronize
pedagogue
pedant
pedestrian
perceptible
perjury
pernicious
philanthropy
philosophical
phosphorescent
photogenic
phototropic
posit
preamble
precept
preclude
predominant
prefigure
privileged
proactive
progenitor
progeny
prohibit
prologue
pronouncement
propel
prospect
protagonist
providential
provocative
rapacious
rapt
recant
recede
recurrent
reform
regress
rejoinder
relapse
relative
renounce
replete
repulsion
resonant
retinue
revival
revoke
semblance
simulate
sophisticate
sophistry
sophomoric
specter
suffuse
superfluous
superlative
surreptitious
susceptible
sustain
symbiotic
synonymous
tenacious
theocracy
translucent

travesty
unanimous
uniform
unison
vestment
vivacious
vivid
voracious

Book IV
aberrant
abject
acerbic
acquisitive
acrid
acrimonious
adherent
admonition
adverse
advocate
aesthetic
anatomy
anesthetic
annotate
antipathy
apathetic
apolitical
apparition
approbation
arrogant
arrogate
aspect
benediction
cautionary
cautious
circumvent
civic
civility
civilize
clamorous
colloquial
compel
complacent
comportment
compunction
conciliatory
concise
conducive
confer
confide
congress
conjecture
connotation
conscientious
constructive
construe
convene
convoluted
correspond
cosmopolitan
counsel
covenant
credence
credible
credulity
crucial
crucible
crux

culpable
culprit
cursory
declaim
decriminalize
deduce
defer
deference
definitive
deflect
degrade
dejected
demagogue
demographic
denotation
deprecate
derogatory
despondent
destitute
deviate
diaphanous
dictate
diffident
diffuse
diligent
dismissive
disparate
dispute
disreputable
dissolute
dissuade
docile
doctrine
doleful
dolorous
dubious
effervescent
effusive
egress
eloquent
emissary
emote
empathy
envisage
epiphany
epitome
equivocate
errant
erroneous
espouse
evince
evocative
evolve
exacerbate
excise
exclamatory
excruciating
exonerate
expel
expound
extort
facile
facsimile
factotum
fallacious
fallacy
fallible
fervent

fervor
fidelity
fractious
gratuitous
imperative
impervious
impetuous
impetus
imprecation
impulse
impute
incautious
incisive
incoherent
incredulous
incriminate
incursion
indoctrinate
indolent
indubitable
induce
inference
infinite
infinitesimal
inflection
inflexible
infraction
infrastructure
infringe
ingrate
ingratiate
inherent
innovative
inquisitive
insoluble
intact
intemperate
interrogate
intractable
introspective
invincible
irrational
locution
malediction
mea culpa
motif
motive
novel
novice
obviate
onerous
onus
pandemic
pathos
penultimate
perspicacious
persuasion
petulant
phenomenon
placebo
placid
politicize
precarious
precaution
precursor
premonition
prescient
presentiment

primacy
primal
primeval
proffer
proficient
profuse
proliferate
proponent
protracted
provincial
punctilious
pungent
purported
rationale
rationalize
recollect
reconcile
recourse
recrimination
redoubtable
remiss
repose
reprobate
reprove
requisition
resolute
restitution
retort
retract
retrospective
revert
sacrilege
sentient
sentiment
sentinel
stature
subvert
sycophant
tactile
tangible
temper
temperance
tome
tortuous
ultimate
ultimatum
unconscionable
viaduct
virile
virtue
virtuoso
visage
voluble

Book V
abominable
abomination
accede
acclivity
acquiesce
adorn
adventitious
ambiance
annex
antecedent
appall
append
appraise

appreciable
apropos
ascertain
assertion
attrition
auspices
auspicious
bacchanal
bacchic
belabor
candid
candor
catholic
certitude
circuitous
communal
conferment
conflagration
congested
consort
consortium
consummate
contort
contravene
contrite
converge
declivity
decorous
decorum
demerit
demonstrative
denigrate
depose
deracinate
desolate
destine
desultory
detrimental
detritus
discomfit
disconcert
disseminate
dissertation
distort
diverge
divulge
ecstasy
edification
elaborate
elegiac
elegy
entity
eradicate
essence
euphoria
excommunicate
exertion
expendable
extant
exultant
feasible
festoon
fete
flagrant
flamboyant
florid
flourish

formality
formulaic
formulate
fortuitous
fortuity
fulminate
germane
germinal
germinate
gestate
gesticulate
hoi polloi
holistic
illustrative
illustrious
impair
impeccable
impending
implicit
importunate
importune
incandescent
incendiary
incense
incommunicado
inexplicable
inflammatory
inordinate
insinuate
insufferable
interject
inundate
irradicable
jocose
jocular
laborious
languid
languish
languor
lenient
lenitive
lethargy
liaison
ligature
liturgy
livid
luster
magnum opus
malaise
malfeasance
malign
malinger
meretricious
meritorious
metaphrase
modus operandi
mollify
monosyllabic
monotone
monotonous
munificent
negate
negligent
negligible

nexus
obligatory
ominous
opulent
ordain
ornate
pallid
pallor
paradigm
paraphrase
parcel
parse
parvenu
peccadillo
peccant
pejorative
periphery
phraseology
plaint
plaintive
polyglot
polymath
precedent
predestine
preferential
preordained
proclivity
propitiate
propitious
quintessence
quittance
rapport
redound
refulgent
remonstrate
remunerate
repartee
requiem
resilient
restive
rudiment
rudimentary
sedition
semantic
seminal
semiotic
sinuous
soliloquy
solipsism
somnolent
sopor
soporific
stanch
stasis
static
staunch
subjective
suborn
summation
surfeit
synergy
totalitarian
totality
transient

transitional
transitory
trenchant
trite
truncate
undulate
verdant
verdure
vigilant
vigilante
viridity
vulgar

Book VI
abscond
abstruse
adduce
adjourn
adjudicate
adroit
adumbrate
aggregate
agrarian
alacrity
allocate
allude
amoral
anachronism
anathema
animadversion
aperture
apocryphal
apposite
apprise
artifice
artless
ascribe
aspire
assay
asset
attenuate
avocation
bucolic
capitulate
caprice
celerity
chronicle
circumlocution
circumscribe
cogent
cognate
colloquy
collusion
complicit
composite
comprise
concede
concordance
consign
conspire

constrain
contend
context
contiguous
contingent
covert
cryptic
defray
degenerate
demise
demur
demure
derisive
devoid
diabolical
discern
discordant
discrete
discretion
discursive
distend
diurnal
dour
duplicitous
duress
dystopian
egregious
emblematic
emulate
engender
ensue
episodic
epithet
esprit
evanescent
execrable
exigent
expiate
explicate
extemporaneous
extenuating
feign
felicitous
felicity
fictive
flux
fruition
fruitless
genre
gregarious
hyperbole
icon
iconoclast
iconography
idyllic
impious
implicate
in lieu of
inanimate
incessant
incite
inconsolable
incorrigible
incurious

inert
inexplicable
infelicitous
infrangible
inimitable
innate
innocuous
insatiable
insuperable
intercede
interlude
internecine
interpose
intransigent
intrusive
inveigh
irrepressible
judicious
locus
loquacious
ludicrous
magniloquent
methodical
moratorium
mores
morose
myopic
nascent
obdurate
obloquy
obsequious
obtrusive
ostensible
overt
parturient
pastoral
peregrination
perpetuate
perpetuity
pertinacious
perturb
plenary
plenipotentiary
portend
precipitate
prestige
pretext
procure
proscribe
proviso
psyche
psychosomatic
psychotic
purveyor
purview
pusillanimous
recapitulate
recondite
rectify
rectitude
refract
remit
repast
repertory

reprehensible
reprimand
reserved
resignation
resuscitate
reticent
risible
rustic
sacrosanct
salubrious
salutary
salutation
satiety
sectarian
segue
servile
signatory
sinecure
sojourn
solace
solicitous
sovereign
stricture
stringent
subdue
subjugate
subservient
subtext
succor
suffrage
suppress
surfeit
surmise
synchronous
synod
synopsis
tacit
taciturn
temporal
temporize
tenable
tendentious
tenet
tenuous
topical
traduce
transect
transfigure
transpire
turbid
turbulent
umbrage
univocal
utopian
vacuity
vacuous
vaunted
vehement
verbatim
verbiage
verbose
vocation
vociferous